The WORD at the Crossings

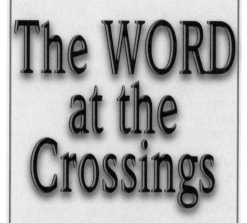

The WORD at the Crossings

Living the Good News in a Multicontextual Community

Eric H. F. Law

CHALICE
PRESS

ST. LOUIS, MISSOURI

Bible quotations, unless otherwise noted, are from the *New Revised Standard Version* Bible, copyright 1989, Division of Christian Education of the National Council of the Churches of Christ in the United States of America. Used by permission. All rights reserved.

Cover art: ©SuperStock
Art direction: Michael Domínguez
Cover design: Mike Foley
Interior design: Hui-chu Wang

This book is printed on acid-free, recycled paper.

Visit Chalice Press on the World Wide Web at
www.chalicepress.com

10   9   8   7   6   5   4   3   2   1   04   05   06   07   08   09

Library of Congress Cataloging–in–Publication Data
Law, Eric H. F.
  The Word at the crossings : living the good news in a multicontextual community / Eric H. F. Law.— 1st ed.
    p. cm.
Includes bibliographical references.
  ISBN 0-8272-4244-1 (alk. paper)
    1. Preaching. 2. Christian education. 3. Pluralism (Social sciences) I. Title.
  BV4221.L39 2004
  251—dc21   2004012260

Printed in the United States of America

Contents

For Walter Wink and Pierre Babin,
and all the preachers and teachers who led me to
the crossings to encounter God again and again.

Acknowledgments

There have been many preachers and teachers whom I have encountered in my life and whose ministries have inspired much of the content of this book. I give thanks to John Snow for simply inviting me to read the whole Bible to prepare for my ordination examination, to Martin Smith for being a wonderful spiritual director while I was in seminary, to George Hunter for listening to me when I was confused at the crossings, to Everett Simpson for his steady and focused advice during my early years in the ordained ministry, to Albany To for preaching two sermons for two different cultural groups in one worship service, to Benjamin and Phoebe Pao for showing me their passion for ministry in the Chinese American cultural environment, to Gurdon Brewster for being there at the most critical crossing of my life, to David Siegenthaler for asking the right question at the right time, to Richard Clifford for opening my eyes to experience the Hebrew Scriptures, to Chester Talton and Jon Bruno for trusting in my ability to teach in the Diocese of Los Angeles, and to Catherine Roskam for her faith in me as a fellow teacher and minister. I am also grateful for the ministry of Kirkridge, where I encountered such wonderful teachers as Walter Wink, Bob Raines, Carter Heyward, Beverly Harrison, John McNeil, Virginia Mollenkott, William Stringfellow, John Boswell, and Daniel Barrigan. I give thanks to all the church communities that have extended their invitations for me to teach and preach in the last twenty years. These experiences are the backbone of this book. As always, I thank Kent Steinbrenner for his proofreading skill. I am especially grateful to Steve Rutberg for his understanding during the stressful times while I struggled to write this book last year. This book took much more time to write than I had expected, and therefore I thank David Polk, my editor, and the people at Chalice Press for their patience and understanding.

Introduction

During the years I was serving in a Chinese American Episcopal Church, I often struggled with preaching and teaching during the Lenten season. The Chinese lunar calendar often dates the Chinese New Year around the first week of Lent. I grew up loving the celebration of the Chinese New Year, with all its festive food and activities, its language of celebration, the positive outlook it engendered, and the joyous well-wishing to family and friends. I was also trained as a priest to value and appreciate the liturgical movement from Lent to Easter as set forth by the church calendar. The church calendar said I should repent, while my Chinese cultural calendar said I should celebrate. How should I teach the gospel in the midst of these conflicting themes?

I had a number of options. I could forget Lent for another week and just celebrate the Chinese New Year with the church community. This was very tempting, but my love for the church would not allow me to do that, even though I knew full well that the church calendar was designed to favor the European cultural calendar. I often felt that if the church calendar were designed by the Chinese, we would probably move Lent up a few more weeks and make Easter coincide with the Chinese New Year, so that when we celebrate the coming of spring in China, we are also celebrating the resurrection of Christ. While this reasoning was valid and would make a very good academic discussion (I actually wrote a paper for my liturgy course in seminary on this subject), this was not realistic in terms of the unity of the church.

Another option would be to tone down the Chinese New Year celebration in favor of the church calendar. This was never an option, because the Chinese New Year was too important for the Chinese community to be put in second place. My third option was to keep the two totally separate. For example, we could do the Lenten ritual in the sanctuary with little reference to the Chinese New Year, and then in the parish hall we could celebrate the Chinese New Year in all its festivity. This, however, would simply reinforce the unhelpful notion that whatever we did in church was to be detached from our everyday lives.

This left me with this final option: to keep the two in tension and preach from the creative crossing of the two. The first thing I would do during the year when the beginning of Lent coincided with the Chinese New Year would be to name the conflict. In naming it, I would then be free to allow either perspective to affirm, enrich, or challenge the other. For example, Lent as a time of self-examination in the Western Christian tradition might be used to affirm and expand the Chinese tradition of cleaning the house before the first day of the year, as well as other rituals that invite the family to examine the previous year's accomplishments and learning as a way to prepare for the New Year. The Chinese New Year tradition of visiting all our friends and relatives to bring well wishes and gifts could be a challenge to the individualistic approach of Lent as a time of giving up something. The Chinese New Year traditions that focus on the community might be used to push Christians to look outward and be aware of the needs of the community—the collective. In the crossing of the two very different traditions, we might come to learn more and to appreciate the strengths and weaknesses of each tradition. More importantly, at the crossing, there is the opportunity to widen our understanding of the gospel.

In writing drama, a scene comes alive where there is tension created by conflict among and within the characters in the scene. People pay attention when they are caught up in how the characters struggle to find resolutions to the conflicts that they face. (This is one of the reasons why I have included a number of dramatic dialogues in this book. They are illustrations of how to work effectively with the tensions of conflict while moving toward resolution. They also can be used as tools for teaching and preaching.) When we name the conflicts among our societal, personal, communal, and gospel values, people in our Christian community pay attention. They want to know how to resolve this conflict so that they can live as faithful followers of Christ. In order to be relevant in Christian community, all Christians need to work through the tension and the conflict in the life of the community and arrive at a "holy" resolution—that which brings us closer to God's will.

In the Chinese language, the word for "crisis" is a compound word consisting of the words for "danger" and "opportunity." In that sense, where there is a crisis—the crossing of differences—there is always the danger of a destructive outcome, in which one group dominates the other or wins, and the other group submits or surrenders. Sometimes both groups are hurt. However, if we approach the crisis constructively, there are opportunities for growth and change. You will find this recurring theme as you read this book: the call to resist the destructive approach to resolving our differences. Instead, let us follow Christ's way in which we treat one another as children of God—brothers and sisters in Christ—even when we consider others as enemies. When we follow Christ's way, we can move the conflict from the legalistic, political, win-lose approach to a compassionate sacred place where love is the driving force leading to possible reconciliation.

Jesus often said, "You have heard that it was said…but I say to you." He named the conflict and invited people to choose that which is God's. The resolution often comes when we realize how our own values and actions do not follow God's will and nature, or how our societal values might be in conflict with God's. The mediator at the crossing of the differences is Christ. Christ may affirm the conviction that we already have. Christ may help us see the situation and issue in a new way, therefore pointing us to a new and unexpected direction. Christ may confront and judge us for turning away from God and challenge us to repent and return to God. Proclaiming the good news has to do with how we can name conflict and invite others to enter the crossings of different value systems, yearnings, and choices, and then enable our communities to recognize the presence of Christ—to find the path to follow Christ and to walk humbly with God.

As you read the chapters in this book, some of you might notice that I am reemphasizing processes and concepts that I have described previously. You might ask, "Is Eric repeating himself?" The answer to that question is, "Yes, I am." I am breaking one of the rules I have learned in writing in the English language, which is to be concise and to the point, not wasting words and pages repeating what has already been said. But every time I started a new chapter of this book, I thought I was onto something new. With great excitement, I followed the thread of my thoughts, only to be disappointed at the end to find that I had returned to the same conclusion again and again. Instead of trying to fight this, I have decided that these recurring themes, patterns, and processes must be what I am supposed to write and teach. I have discovered that when I utilize these repeated patterns in my teaching and preaching, I have a better chance of putting the gospel forward in new and relevant ways. I use these repeated patterns to plan my sermons. I apply these repeated processes when I facilitate a meeting or teach class. Each time I come around to writing about the same theme and pattern, I get a clearer and deeper understanding of these processes that I have been using and teaching. In fact, I actually live my life according to these patterns.

When preparing to enter as a Christian into a multicultural environment, I often found myself lost in the task of deciding what to say. What do I preach in a community in which there are people with opposing points of view? What do I teach in a setting where people come from very different upbringings with diverging emphases in their views of family/individual, relations, and power? What do I say to help a community make sense of living in a multicultural, pluralistic world/society? The "what" questions assume a model of teaching and preaching that puts the teacher/preacher in a position of someone who knows, and who regards the listeners and students as people who do not know. The teacher/preacher's job is to impart knowledge to the listeners/students. With this limited assumption of teacher-student and preacher-listener relationships, I would not know what would be the right thing to say or do if I were to value all the different experiences and perspectives residing in the people of my community. As it was impossible for me to know all the different cultural contexts in my community, I could not really say with certainty that what I taught or preached would connect to them. Perhaps asking the "what" question might be the wrong initial approach when preparing to teach and preach in a pluralistic environment.

As I struggled to discern how to share the gospel in a pluralistic world, I began to see more clearly that it is not a matter of *what* I teach, but *how* I teach. The process of arriving at the preaching moment is as important as the final sermon. The process that I use to teach is as significant as the content of the lesson. The more useful question I have found myself asking when I plan my sermons or agenda for a meeting or a class is: Does the process that I use follow the pattern of Christ's way, truth, and life?

My invitation to you is to come along with me and struggle to clarify this process that seeks to align ourselves with God. This journey is, first of all, personal. Throughout the book, especially in chapter 1, I have included personal experiences as ways to get at what I am trying to say. This personal exploration is an essential part of the discipline for all Christians in a pluralistic environment. One must know oneself as much as possible in order to communicate the gospel authentically and passionately. You are invited to explore your own stories, assumptions, frameworks, and God-concepts as I have shared mine. It would be a good idea to keep a journal as you read this book and do some of the suggested exercises after each chapter.

This journey is biblical. We will come back to the Bible again and again because the Bible "contains all things necessary for salvation." It is the source we Christians look to in order to pattern our work and our lives after God's nature and will. Chapters 2 and 3 explore how we are to live with the Bible in its pluralistic context. You are invited to read the Bible regularly as you read this book. My suggestion is for you to follow the common lectionary and read the lessons for the upcoming Sunday. Write down your reflections as you connect with these texts.

This journey is dialogical. In some ways this book is a dialogue among the key parties at the crossing of differences—personal, communal, societal, and biblical. Dialogue at these crossings will point the way toward God through Christ. For this reason, I have included a number of plays in the book. As I learned more about my own internal culture and that of other persons and groups, I found that different parts of myself are in dialogue with one another as I explore different issues at the crossings. Writing plays—constructing dialogue among different fictional characters expressing different perspectives—is my way of working out these conflicts and tensions at the crossing. It forces me to put myself in others' skin and to feel, see, and articulate their experiences as closely as possible to how they would themselves. You are invited to write dialogue between different parts of yourself, and to record dialogue with other persons and groups who might have different perspectives. This is part of the journey to discovering the truth (chapter 4). In order to continue to testify to the truth, you are invited to further explore the different powers and forces at work in our lives and institutions that might cause us to alienate ourselves away from God again. Chapter 5 issues a caution to be aware and work with the "angels" at the crossings.

This journey is practical. Like all my previous books, I have proposed different practical disciplines, models, and techniques for teaching and preaching at the crossings. In particular, I have included a sermon-preparation model in chapter 6 that I have been using for my preaching classes. This model involves listening as a starting point for speaking the truth. The principles in this model deal with preaching, but they are really about any sharing of the gospel whenever Christians proclaim the good news and speak the truth, whether in a sermon or in any other part of life. In chapter 7, I have included descriptions of what I call "a pedagogy of the powerful" and "a pedagogy of the powerless." As we travel along in this journey, I also invite you to try these patterns of teaching the good news in your lives and ministries. These chapters will be of particular interest to you if your Christian ministry involves teaching and preaching—or if these forms of ministry may be in your future. But the principles applied in these chapters are really for everyone. I present patterns and processes for communicating the Christian faith and sharing the gospel in a pluralistic world. All Christians are called to this ministry of sharing the gospel, and so these principles apply to everyone.

These patterns and processes are by no means the ultimate ones. They are but some that I have discovered in my study and experience in ministry. And, as always, this continues to be a dialogue. Your feedback to me is essential for me to continue to learn and grow myself. Therefore, bring your experience, your feelings, your thinking, your community, and your Bible, and come along with me to the crossings.

Prologue

The following is a sermon preached at the chapel of Garrett-Evangelical Theological Seminary during the second week of Lent, 2003.

As I was flipping through the almost-finished manuscript of this book, looking for appropriate material for a sermon for the second week of Lent, I realized that this book was over a year late getting to my publisher. I fully intended to finish the book by Christmas 2001, but like a lot of people, the horrible events of September 11, 2001, had derailed my effort. I literally could not write a word for six months. Everything I thought about writing down seemed trivial and insignificant. Finally, in February 2002, I informed my editor, who was gracious and understanding, that I would not be able to deliver the book for at least another six months, if not a year.

Writing is like breathing for me. The breathing out must be accompanied by breathing in. I was forcing myself to breathe out too much—to produce—and forgetting to give myself time and space to breathe in. My creativity was suffocating, and therefore, I could not write. Having removed the pressure to produce a completed book, I decided to do some breathing in for the year 2002. "Breathing in" means observing, taking in the information, the small details of life, both in me and around me, and keeping an eye and ear on the big picture of what is happening in our communities, in our nations, and in the world. As soon as I stopped forcing myself to be in the doing mode, I began to see, hear, and feel in ways that surprised and challenged me. But most importantly, my listening and observing also affirmed the topic of this book: How to preach and teach the good news in a multicontextual community.

Here are some of the things I saw, heard, and felt in the year 2002, leading up to the second week of Lent in the year 2003. The list below is by no means a complete list, nor is it objective. It is not organized in any profound or logical way. It is just a cloud of things—some heartwarming, some disturbing, some challenging, some confusing—all floating in my head, sometimes all at once, and sometimes in amplified, concentrated forms.

I saw the outpouring of goodwill from many people, people who gave their money, time, and energy in support of the families of victims who died in the attacks. I felt the tears and pride as people honored the heroes and heroines who gave up their lives in order to save others. I spent sleepless nights wondering whether I would have the courage to give my life up for others if I were in the same situation as those people in the hijacked planes or facing the burning towers. I saw people taking more notice of their families and loved ones—staying home more instead of traveling, and spending quality time with one another.

I saw a powerful nation suddenly realizing that it was not as secure as it liked to think. I felt the humiliation of being picked out of line at the airport and being searched while my fellow citizens watched and questioned my character in their heads. All the while I was also glad that we were taking precautions in making sure that there were no terrorists boarding my plane. I found myself clutching my United States passport like a badge of courage when I traveled in my own homeland as proof that I belonged. I heard people saying that they were willing to give up some of their civil liberty in order to have security. I heard people saying that what little civil liberty they had left was being taken away in the name of security.

I saw people around me and in the media suddenly claiming to be patriotic to their nation. I saw people who advocated for the understanding of those who hated us being shut out of conversations. I heard people in another nation cheering over the destruction of an icon of success in my country. I saw a powerful nation that suffered a great loss and shock deciding to retaliate with military force against another nation. I felt judged as being unpatriotic when I spoke against war and violence as the only response to violence. I saw neighbors watching neighbors with suspicion because they did not see a U.S. flag displayed on the front porch.

I felt an overwhelming sadness when I got out of the New York subway station and instinctively looked up to find the Twin Towers in order to determine which way was south, and then remembered that the towers were no more. I felt totally incompetent trying to say anything intelligent to a group of church members in New York City. I felt the calloused hands of volunteers who tirelessly dug for months at the World Trade Center site to recover the remains of those who died. I saw people moving through rituals that respected the dignity of those who died.

I saw an already decimated country being bombed in the name of liberating the oppressed women and children in that country. I saw a war-torn country liberated and a transitional government put into place, giving hope for the people. I saw a frustrated nation not being able to capture and eliminate the "evil one." I saw a powerful nation in fear of being attacked again. I saw a nation ignoring the need of a destroyed nation and shifting its focus to another enemy. I saw large corporations cheating and leaving countless people without financial security, losing their investments and pensions in the process, and my government moving very slowly to address this injustice. I saw the price of gasoline going up more than 50 percent—and yet still I pumped it into my car.

I saw young soldiers leaving their families and loved ones to prepare for war. I heard the talk of waging war as a means to protect our nation. I heard people complaining that my nation was waging a war for oil. I heard people defending our right to protect ourselves and that it therefore justified a preemptive strike. I heard that someone got arrested for wearing a T-shirt that said, "Give Peace a Chance." I saw poets writing peace poetry and reading them in coffeehouses and bookstores. I heard chanting for peace from thousands of students at college and high school campuses. I saw the passion for peace and the zeal for war flaring up in opposition between young people and not-so-young people. I saw my church in a regional convention attempting to pass an anti-war resolution, but ending up backing off from making a stand because some people said that making a stand against war would divide the church.

At the crossing of being victims and aggressors, at the crossing of justice as retaliation and justice as fairness to all involved, at the crossing of the need for security and the need to honor civil liberty, at the crossing of conformity in the name of patriotism and the freedom of speech that is as much the heart of my country, at the crossing of the just war theory and pacifism, at the crossing of conquering the evil ones and the command to love our enemy, how shall I preach and teach the gospel of Jesus Christ? Where is the good news? How can we discern what is God's will when God's blessing is being claimed by opposing sides? How can we sing the Lord's song in this land so full of opposing passions?

> Then [Jesus] began to teach them that the Son of Man must undergo great suffering, and be rejected by the elders, the chief priests, and the scribes, and be killed, and after three days rise again...And Peter took him aside and began to rebuke him. But turning and looking at his disciples, he rebuked Peter and said, "Get behind me, Satan! For you are setting your mind not on divine things but on human things." (Mk. 8:31–33)

Peter rebuked Jesus because Peter only heard partially what Jesus was saying. He heard only the great suffering, the rejection, the dying. He had set his mind on "human things" and therefore only heard the human part of the prediction. Perhaps, like Peter, my paralysis had to do with my setting my mind on human things only. When I set my mind solely on human things, I saw how small and insignificant I was as one person. One person in the midst of all the other human things that were happening in my country, and across the Atlantic, and in the Middle East. When I only saw human things, I became frightened. I was afraid of what others might think of me if I really said what I believed. I was afraid of becoming an irrelevant, out-of-touch writer if I did not write a book that addressed the event of 9/11 directly. I was afraid that if I really let myself feel the pain of those who died and their loved ones who survived, I would fall so deep into the abyss of depression that I would never find my way out. My preoccupation with being liked, being strong, being right, and being a hero were but human things. My inability to write was just a human thing. My fear was a human thing.

How, then, can I set my mind on divine things at times like these? I begin with what Peter did not hear in Jesus' prediction—in three days, Jesus will rise again. So, to set my mind on divine things is to know the whole story of Jesus, which includes the assurance of the resurrection. If Peter had heard and understood that there would be a resurrection, he would not have rebuked Jesus concerning his suffering. To know that there will be a resurrection is what gives me courage to endure the suffering, the confusion, the dark tunnel that does not seem to have a light at the end. Now that I know the end of the story, which is resurrection and not death, I can go back to the beginning of the story to learn about divine things.

In the gospel of Luke, we are told that there was no room at the inn and that Mary had to give birth to Jesus in a cave outside of town. Only the lowly shepherds and the animals were there to greet the newborn Jesus. Perhaps we have no room for the divine thing, which is Jesus, in our hearts and in the society in which we live today. Only the powerless in our world, like the shepherds at the beginning of Jesus' earthly ministry, responded and saw the divine thing happening in their midst. Perhaps the first step in setting my mind on divine things is to listen to the powerless in our society.

In the gospel according to Matthew, we are told that Herod sought to kill Jesus, and Mary, Joseph, and Jesus had to escape in secret to Egypt, going into exile. Perhaps we too need to know that we are in exile as Christians at this time, because we are living in a world that does not speak the same language as we Christians speak. We are experiencing a world that does not value the same things we Christians value. We need to acknowledge that we are indeed in exile in our homeland. We then need to connect with others who are also in exile. In listening and sharing with other powerless outcasts, we may begin to find our way back to the crossing with renewed vision and energy, instead of paralysis.

A couple of months after the destruction of the World Trade Center, I was doing a workshop at a church on Park Avenue in New York City. Leaders from churches in the greater New York City area came to this workshop after it had been postponed due to the tragic events of September 11, 2001. All through the week leading up to this event, I struggled with how to teach and what to teach, when the national context had been irreversibly altered. I dreaded having to face this group of people whose lives had been directly impacted by the destruction of their city's icon—not to mention the loss of relatives and friends. Where was the good news in the midst of their grief, confusion, disbelief, and anger?

As people arrived that morning, I did not sense the usual energy for learning that I got from other groups. Instead, I noticed that their minds seemed to be somewhere else. This was, no doubt, one of those humbling experiences. As I was being introduced as an internationally known author and teacher in building inclusive community, I felt completely incompetent. The workshop on congregational development I had prepared to do seemed irrelevant and trivial. Right before I stood up to address the group, I decided to discard the program I had planned. I stood up and began to share my apprehension, confusion, and sense of inadequacy with the group. Then I invited the group to step back, and I asked them not to worry about the subject and content of the workshop today. Instead, I suggested they spend some time focusing on God—the divine thing. I facilitated a Bible study process in which each person was invited to share his or her reflections on the scriptural passage from the upcoming lectionary texts. The Hebrew Scripture was Exodus 12:21–28, concerning the final instructions for the first Passover. The Bible study involved reading the same passage three times. After the first reading, participants were invited to share a word or phrase that stood out for them. After the second reading, participants were invited to reflect and share on this question: How does this passage connect with your life and ministry? After the third reading, they were invited to explore the question: What does God invite you to do, to be, or to change through this passage?

Then I sat down and I listened. Almost everyone talked about personal experiences of the September 11 event. Not only that, they connected their experiences with God through listening to the biblical text. There were certainly very different and diverging perspectives, but sharing them in the context of reflecting on scripture enabled the participants to listen and respect one another's experiences. At the end of the Bible study process, many participants told me that this was the first time they had had a real dialogue about their experiences with anyone. Furthermore, some participants said that this was the first time they had been able to tell how they really felt about all this as Christians, without the fear that someone would judge them as being unpatriotic. And everyone felt relieved and released from the burden that they had been carrying since September 11. As a result of the Bible study, they now had a clearer sense of what they needed to do next.

At this gathering of exiled Christians, we stopped what we were supposed to be doing and stepped back and reconnected with God. We did that by reading scripture together and recalling the saving acts of God in our lives. We set our minds back on divine things. We recalled, through reading scripture, how we were once slaves and how God had delivered us from bondage to freedom. In the process we returned to the crossing with a clearer sense of direction.

This is the invitation in this time of conflicting passions and confusing values. To set our minds on divine things begins with stopping what we are doing and breathing in a little and remembering God's acts of salvation in history through God's promises to Adam and Eve, to Noah, to Abraham and Sarah; God's liberating acts in delivering Israel out of slavery; and God's challenge to Israel to stay faithful. Most importantly, we recall the story of how Jesus fulfilled God's promise, and his challenge to us through his word and actions.

In reviewing these stories, we might discover anew the pattern of how God, through Christ, sees and acts in the world. We then return to the crossing with fresh eyes to see as Jesus would see, with clear ears to listen as Jesus would listen, with true words to speak as Jesus would speak. To set our minds on divine things is to be able to see, feel, and act in the world as God, through Christ, sees, feels, and acts in it. To set our minds on divine things is to know that Christ is the way, the truth, and the life. To set our minds on divine things is to follow Christ all the way to the cross. To set our minds on divine things is to know that in dying, we will have new life. To set our minds on divine things is to know with certainty that on the third day, Christ is risen indeed.

With that assurance, we are called to endure and be faithful. We are called to connect with the powerless and the exiled and find our ways together. We are called to return to the crossings with courage and clarity in what we say and do. We can have the courage to speak the truth as we hear it and the courage to listen to the truth as others speak it. We can have the courage to act with passion for the truth that is the divine thing. With that assurance, I know that, as Paul said:

> *I am convinced that neither death, nor life, nor angels, nor rulers, nor things present, nor things to come, nor powers, nor height, nor depth, nor anything else in all creation, will be able to separate us from the love of God in Christ Jesus our Lord. (Rom. 8:38–39)*

Amen.

CHAPTER 1

Encountering God Anew
at the Crossings

"Write a biography of God-concepts in your life." This was the first assignment I gave to a group of experienced pastors and priests who came for a one-week intensive seminar on the subject "Preaching in a Multicultural Community." I explained the assignment this way: "In the act of preaching, we are working with people's God-images and concepts—evoking them, reclaiming them, affirming them, challenging them, shaping them, reshaping them, and changing them. In order to do this task faithfully, we have to first recover how our own God-concepts have evolved and changed in our lives over the years. In other words, you are invited to explore how God interacted with you during different periods in your lives. In the revelation of God or the in-breaking of the Holy Spirit at significant moments in your lives, you may have been given opportunities to connect with God at a different point and therefore may have gained a view of a different dimension of God. In the process, we might discover what God-concept drives our teaching and preaching, and from where our passion for ministry came."

In other words, this is an exercise for all Christians. It's something we need to do as the first step in our process of learning to communicate the gospel in a pluralistic world.

As a rule, I have never asked my students to do anything I have not done myself. The following was the result of my reflection on this assignment.

15

"If you look at anyone with lust, you have already committed adultery in your heart." Father Jung paraphrased a saying attributed to Jesus from Matthew 5:28. I was a fifth-grade student in a Roman Catholic school in Hong Kong. Sitting in my weekly Bible class, I was terrified that I had broken one of the Ten Commandments, even though I had no idea what adultery was. However, I did have some inkling of what looking at someone with lust was about. Whatever Father Jung said, you believed. In the Chinese language, we called a Roman Catholic priest "Shun Fu," which literally means "God Father." With a title like that, he had to be the representative of God. Having seen pictures of God depicted as an old man with a long white beard, I was convinced that God was like a father or a grandfather. Besides, Jesus called God his father. What more proof did I need?

I was the youngest of six children. By the time I was born, my father might have lost interest in babies. I did not remember my father ever holding me or playing with me when I was little. My father was someone I talked to through my mother whenever I needed his signature for my report card or a permission form to go on a field trip. As the youngest, I also observed my father reprimanding all my older siblings when they did something wrong. He would go on for hours recounting everything that they had done wrong from the day that they were born. The "father" concept of God as taught in my Bible class fitted well with my experience of my father—distanced, authoritative, a permission-giver, a rule-setter. The scariest part of that is that if God were like my father, he would also possess a very long memory of everything that I had ever done wrong. As proofs to these ideas of God, we also studied the stories of Adam and Eve, the tower of Babel, the flood, and Lot's wife. They all pointed to the punishing disciplinarian Father-God.

I am sure that Father Jung also taught us many stories of Jesus' love and God's grace. But living in a culture that emphasized the authority of the elders and the importance of the collective—the family and the community—I obviously paid more attention to the concepts of God that reinforced the dominant cultural values of the society in which I lived. I also remember spending a lot of time in Bible class on the Fifth Commandment: Honor your father and mother. In Chinese literature classes, we were also taught the importance of filial piety. I remember vividly my teacher reciting a verse from Confucius that went something like this: "If the father wanted the son to die and the son did not die, that would be considered disrespectful." In the Chinese cultural mind-set, Jesus was the ultimate example of a good son who obeyed his Father's demand for him to die. Father Jung also pointed out the significance of Jesus' mother at the foot of the cross. He died for his family and for the good of the larger community.

When I was fourteen, my family immigrated to the United States of America and settled in New York City. One of the first places we visited was the Episcopal Mission in Chinatown. The familiarity of church was a comfort that we needed desperately in the foreign environment. The mission was still in its infant stage of development, and we were invited to be part of the ministries right away. My oldest brother was on the Bishop's Committee. All my siblings got summer jobs at the church. After the first year, for some political reason, the priest left, and so did the organist. The new priest arrived and immediately reaffirmed my family's involvement with the ongoing ministry of the mission. At the age of fifteen, I was naïve enough to agree to be the organist, even though I had never played one before. My piano-playing skills did not prepare me for playing the organ, but I did okay and the church community was very forgiving. The positive side of this new role was that I had to be in church every Sunday.

Our new priest, Father To, preached two different sermons each Sunday—one in English for the young people, and one in Chinese. I found the Chinese sermon boring and irrelevant, but his English sermon was interesting and engaging, even though I was struggling to become proficient in the English language during that time. Father To was also enrolled in a master's degree program in business administration, and what he was learning in business school worked its way into his English sermon and teaching. Through school and the media, mainly television, I was absorbing a set of cultural values and patterns that emphasized the personal and individual. Therefore, I was fascinated by Father To's use of the language of commerce and individual gain or loss. When he preached a sermon about the "cost" of our salvation and that God had "paid" for my "individual" salvation by offering his son, I was sold. This way of thinking about God and myself was exciting to me because it helped me survive in the new culture in which I found myself. God was a businessman trading his son's life for mine, and that made sense for the time being.

I went to college at Cornell University, away from my family and the urban environment of New York City. According to the new cultural values I was absorbing in the United States, I was supposed to find myself, do my own thing, and be independent by the time I turned eighteen. The first place on campus I visited was the Episcopal Campus Ministry. There I found the full version of individualistic Christianity. God was no longer an entity "out there" lording it over me. God was a loving parent—not just a father but also a mother—who paid attention to me as an important person, beloved and empowered. God incarnated through Christ. We are the body of Christ. God therefore incarnated in me. God was in me. I was in communion with God. In that communion, I was called to be creative, to work for justice, and to love everyone around me. I called my priest, Gurdon Brewster, by his first name—no more of the formality that came with a distanced, high-up-in-the-sky God. The campus ministry community also introduced me to God as feminine, which opened me up to a new horizon of relating to women in my life, especially my mother. God as a mother made so much more sense to me because my mother was the parent who was always there for me. She could almost always anticipate my needs before I had to ask for them.

I am sure that Gurdon and the church community leaders at Cornell taught on many occasions about the importance of community and the collective. Immersing myself in the exciting culture of individualism, I did not pay much attention to these ideas but focused and claimed those theological ideas that supported my individualistic yearnings.

A parallel development of this inward journey was an outward path to nature. Cornell University is built on top of a hill, surrounded by the beauty of nature in Ithaca, New York— waterfalls, magnificent gorges, big old trees of every kind, multicolored foliage in the fall, and blossoming trees in the spring. Every year, I was invited to go on retreats and commune with nature, where I was introduced to the idea that God was in nature.

God not only created me personally, God also made this wonderful and wondrous creation, full of lessons and mysteries. I was called to take care of this creation on behalf of God—its original creator. If I were to be in communion with God, I had to be in communion with nature as well. The lyrics of a song I wrote during that time depicted my idea of God well:

> Praise the God of all Creation
> Alleluia
> Praise the same God in our hearts
> Alleluia

These ideas of God, incarnate both in persons and in nature, were a perfect match of my experience of being in a highly individualistic, competitive environment as well as a place surrounded by the beauty of nature. I held tight to these ideas of God through college, my first full-time job as a computer systems designer, and my discernment process to eventually seek ordination in the Episcopal Church.

My experience in seminary continued to affirm my egocentric, individualistic approach to my faith. But deep down inside, I began to notice that something was missing. I saw the signs of this "missing something" everywhere I turned while living in the seminary community. There was the prominent and exciting feminist liberation theology group. There was the anti-nuclear arms movement organizing protests and prayer vigils. There was the gay and lesbian support group. There was the seminarians of color group. There were guitar-strumming musicians. There were the organ/choir-loving people. There were daily cocktail parties in a certain professor's apartment to which not everyone was invited. I wanted to be part of all these groups, but I felt the pressure to choose one or the other. For example, during the seminary's struggle to address racism in my first year, as the only Asian American I was caught in the battle between the blacks and the whites, and was left bleeding in the middle—pitied by one group, excluded by the other.

Everywhere I turned there was separation and isolation. Some of these boundaries were defined by others, and some were self-imposed. Little real communication existed among these different camps, and misunderstanding abounded. I saw the danger of the individualistic approach to faith, which might lead to highly specialized groups and individuals claiming they were the ones who had the right answers, while refusing to communicate and understand others' points of view.

Whereas seminary was affirming and exciting in many ways, I found that my concept of God, which was shared by many of my classmates and professors, did not produce the kind of result that I had envisioned for a community of faith. The crisis pushed me toward finding another way to be faithful, and a new concept of God began to emerge. Communication became a major focus for me by the end of my first year in seminary. I began to make the connection between communication and communion. When there was true communication between people, there was God. God was in the connection, and Christ was the medium. My goal in life was to communicate with myself, with others, and with nature.

In a retreat facilitated by a Roman Catholic priest, I learned about a program called Audio-Visual Communication of Faith— a four-month program taught in France. Without giving it a second thought, I sold my car, the only possession I had, and found my way to the Catholic University of Lyon to study with Father Pierre Babin, the founder and director of the program. In this program, we lived in a community that used three languages to communicate—English, French, and Spanish. While studying in this multilingual international environment with students from all over the world, I discovered that I did not get along very well with many of the students, especially the ones from Asia. Because making connections and facilitating true communication was extremely important to me, I tried even harder to communicate with these students. Then they accused me of being too pushy and dominating. What, me—a rude and pushy Chinese? Or was I Chinese? It dawned on me that they were reacting to the "American" part of me. My American individualism had gotten in the way of my ability to build meaningful relationships with others, especially those from Asia.

At the end of the program, I had some personal time with Fr. Babin, who was a very wise person. He said, and I shall never forget, "Eric, you are very talented. But you need to go home to the United States and work with the poor." I had no idea what he meant by that. But I was willing to trust him.

When I returned to seminary that winter, I discovered that the Episcopal Diocese of Massachusetts had started a Chinese Ministry at the Cathedral. Furthermore, I had heard that the ministry had attracted many Chinese refugees and immigrants from Southeast Asia. I thought I would check out this ministry to see if this was a place in which I might consider fulfilling my promise to "work with the poor."

On the first Sunday after I returned to Boston, I went to St. Paul's Cathedral and saw a small group of about twenty-five Chinese sitting in the sanctuary in a semicircle. A Chinese priest, Father Benjamin Pao, presided at the holy eucharist. I heard the gospel being read and proclaimed with such eloquence in Cantonese, it was like I had never heard it before. Indeed, I was hearing and witnessing another way of connecting with God different from my experience of church in college and in seminary. I looked around the circle, and I sensed an intimate connection between the priest and every person, young and old, rich and poor. This connection was in a fatherly way, but was not the father image I had learned in my childhood. While the priest was consecrating the wine and bread, I had an epiphany: I saw and truly believed for the first time that the gospel could be embodied fully in the Chinese language and culture. I began to think of God as possibly having an Asian face. I knew I had to explore this further if I were to be faithful to my calling. I had to recover my Chinese culture as full potential for the embodiment of the gospel of Jesus Christ. I decided to do my field education at the Chinese Ministry. My job was to preach once a month and to help with the ministry to the youth.

Working in the Chinese cultural environment again, I reencountered the God-concepts I learned in my childhood. God as an authoritative, sovereign Lord and Father was very important to this group of people who had lived through the most perilous and unstable experience—war. To have a God who focused on the family and the collective was most significant to people who had lost their family to war and to the immigration experience. My God-image came around in full circle, but the Father-God concept was now bigger and greater than what I had thought before. Now, God was not just a parent based on my assumptions of my own father, but a keeper of the community and a protector of the family. God was revealed when community members, like those of a Chinese family, struggled to stay connected with one another no matter how difficult the situation might be. I started to go home to New York City more often during this period of my life, and I spent time with my parents and began to rebuild our neglected relationships.

Since then, I have devoted my life to the struggle to describe God, making God known every day in different communities. I have learned that God is not limited by my own perception and assumption. God might show a different side of God's self according to the different contexts and communities in which we find ourselves. The revelation of God comes through our struggle to discern where God is and how God affirms or challenges individuals and communities in new contexts and different moments in time.

As I reviewed my own "biography of God-concepts" summarized above, I discovered that each time there was a major change in my life, there was an accompanying change in God-concept. In my class, when my students reported their biographies of God-concepts, they also attested that most of the changes in God-concept came at a major transition or change in their lives. They often began their introduction of a new God-image with:

"When my grandmother died…"
"When I got married…"
"When I had my first child…"
"When I came out as gay man…"
"When my parents moved…"

The scenario of how the revelation of a new dimension of God came to us often involved stepping out, and, in some cases, being forced out, of our comfortable cultural environment and into a different context with sometimes opposing values, beliefs, and assumptions about life, individual, family, community, and God. In my need to survive and to make sense of the new world in which I found myself, I called on a different relationship with God. In the crossing and re-crossing of cultures in my life, different

God-concepts and images emerged to help me adapt, persevere, and stay faithful. At times, the God-image was simply an imposition of the dominant cultural group in order to reinforce the dominant cultural values. At times, the God-image was introduced to me as a way to counter the dominant cultural values. Nevertheless, as I encountered these crossings over time, I matured and began to stand outside of myself and my cultural environment and make the distinctions between my own values, the values of my cultural environment, and God's values. As I did this, I began to discover the many dimensions of God that I did not see from staying in one cultural environment.

This does not mean that I rejected the old idea of God when I received the new one. My perception of God just gained another dimension. God did not cease to be a father when I realized that God could also be like a mother to me. God did not cease to be a Lord who demanded justice when I realized that God was also a loving, merciful parent. God did not cease to be the grandparent who held the community together in unity when I discovered that God was the one who traded Jesus, the Son, for my individual salvation. In the crossing of cultures, personalities, value differences, and theologies, I was given the opportunity to see a greater vision of God.

I am grateful to my parents for having the courage to move from their own familiar environment to the United States, putting me in the middle of the crossing of two divergent cultures. I am thankful for mentors and teachers who have led me to the crossings to encounter nature, to live with people from another nation, to work with people from another economic status. Beyond allowing others to take me to the crossings, I have learned not to be afraid of these crossings of differences, but to courageously seek the opportunities to enter these crossings. In other words, the way to see God more clearly or to respond to God more faithfully is to seek out and encounter others who have a different background and may have a different concept of God. At the crossing of these differences, I am forced to stand outside of myself again and see that my concept of God is but one way, one perspective among many in how people relate to God. At the crossing, I am steered away from the danger of my idolatrous claim that my concept of God is universal. At the crossing, the possibility of the revelation of a fuller vision of God increases as I struggle to reconcile the differences I have with others I encounter. At the crossing, I have a greater chance of staying faithful to God.

At a gathering of theological students, after I gave a lecture on God-concepts similar to what I have written in this chapter, a student asked, "This God-concept is really serious business, isn't it? I'm from Texas and I can remember David Koresh's community in Waco and how his God-concept caused him and his community to come to such a harmful end. And what about Osama bin Laden's God-concept, which he used to justify such terrorism?"

"Yes," I welcomed the opportunity to expound on this theme. "Teaching God-concepts is very serious, and it is dangerous to teach God-concepts in isolation without the benefit of diversity. In both cases that you cited, the leaders had a very narrow idea of God and they taught these limited concepts of God in total isolation. The result can be devastating to the people who are taught that way. Therefore, as people of the church, we have a very serious responsibility in making sure that we teach God-concepts in the context of diversity."

Jesus did not socialize or engage in theological discourse with only one group of people during his early ministry. He did not isolate himself with just the mainstream religious circle of his time, but spent time at the crossings with the poor, women, the outcast, the unclean, tax collectors, Samaritans, and Gentiles. In the crossings of the powerful and the powerless, the clean and the unclean, the intellectuals and the uneducated, the saints and the sinners, the oppressors and the oppressed, death and life, Jesus proclaimed the good news again and again. The gospel came alive and became clearer at each crossing.

Let me go back to the classroom where I had invited my students to share their biographies of God-concepts. After listening to all the reports, which presented a wide spectrum of God-images and concepts, we looked at one another in a moment of amazement. We could hear a collective "wow" in the room. One of the students verbalized our feeling: "Isn't it wonderful that God is so great, so wide, and so adaptive to all of us who had such diverse upbringings and cultural contexts, needs, and struggles?" This same God has many different dimensions and faces. Many of these dimensions are beyond our understanding and comprehension. This understanding of the "greatness" of God is essential in how we live and proclaim the good news at the crossings of diverse cultures that exist in our communities.

"The peace of God, which surpasses all understanding, will guard your hearts and your minds in Christ Jesus" (Phil. 4:7).

Suggested Exercises

1. Write a biography of God-concepts. When finished, examine how wide or narrow your God-concepts have been in your life. How do these God-concepts still influence your teaching and preaching now?

2. If you are a preacher, review the last five sermons you have preached. Pull out the God-concepts used in these sermons. Again, ask how wide or narrow were your uses of God-concepts in your preaching. What can you do to expand the images that you will use for your future sermons? Some suggestions:

    a. Instead of choosing a biblical text to preach on a theme, try using the common lectionary, which "forces" the preacher to read and preach texts that they might not be familiar with. This might challenge the preacher to connect with different images and concepts of God.

    b. Be conscious of the God-concepts that you use for each sermon and over time; make sure that you cover a wider range of images of God in your sermons.

3. If you are a teacher, review that last five lesson plans that you have used. Pull out the God-concepts used in these lesson plans. Again, ask how wide or narrow were your uses of God-concepts in your teaching. What can you do to expand the concepts of God being taught to your class? Some suggestions:

    a. Be conscious of what God-concept is being taught at each lesson and make sure that, over time, a wide range of God-concepts is being covered.

    b. Use a lectionary-based curriculum to ensure a diversity of scriptural texts being studied and therefore present a wider range of God-images.

    c.   Find out what your students' God-concepts are by doing an activity that invites them to share their God images. Enabling your students to listen and appreciate others' God-concepts will go far in helping them appreciate diversity in their midst.

4. Invite others in your church study-group to keep track of the different God-concepts being used in the next three main worship services in your church. What God-concepts or images are used in the hymns, the prayers, the sermon, scriptural readings, announcements, and so forth? Again, ask how wide or narrow the God-concepts being used in your worship services are.

5. Invite your class to take a tour of the church buildings—the sanctuary, the meeting hall, the offices, the kitchen, and so forth. As they move around the building, invite them to keep track of the different God-concepts and images presented in the architecture, the art, the arrangement of the furniture, and other objects in these buildings. Invite them to share how these God-concepts affect their experiences as members of this community. Invite them to reflect on the question, How do these God-concepts impact newcomers to the church positively and/or negatively?

Chapter 2

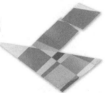

The Bible at the Crossings

We speak of pluralism as if it is something new that we have to contend with in the twenty-first century. But pluralism—and its diversity of experiences, assumptions, perceptions, frameworks, beliefs, and values—has been around for a long time. It was around during Jesus' early ministry and certainly during the formation of the early church. The early Christian church leaders had to address issues raised by pluralism that existed among the believers. Read Acts and you will see how the apostles faced pluralism head-on as they moved the Christian faith beyond the boundary of the Jewish community. Therefore, we do not need to go far to find ways to address pluralism. It was being addressed already in the early church, and we see evidence of this in the final form of the Christian Scriptures. To demonstrate this, I begin this chapter with an imaginary dialogue among four early church leaders in their attempt to address pluralism in Bible—specifically, the four gospels.

The Genealogy Problem—A Play

Time: Early in the formation of the Christian Church

Place: A meeting in which four leaders of the church named Matthew, Luke, Mark, and John discuss an issue around a discrepancy in the Bible.

Wall chart for the play "The Genealogy Problem"

Luke's genealogy	Matthew's genealogy
Adam, Seth, Enos, Cainan, Mahalaleel, Jared, Enoch, Methuselah, Lamech, Noah, Shem, Arphaxad, Cainan, Shelah, Eber, Peleg, Reu, Serug, Nahor, Terah	
Abraham_____	Abraham
Isaac _____	Isaac
Jacob_____	Jacob
Judah_____	Judah *and Tamar*
Perez_____	Perez
Hezron_____	Hezron
Arni	Aram
Admin	
Amminadab _____	Aminadab
Nahshon_____	Nahshon
Sala	Salmon *and Rahab*
Boaz _____	Boaz *and Ruth*
Obed_____	Obed
Jesse_____	Jesse
David _____	David *and wife of Uriah*
Nathan, Mattatha, Menna, Melea, Eliakim,	Solomon
Jonam, Joseph, Judah	Rehoboam
Simeon	Abijah, Asaph
Levi	Jehoshaphat
Matthat	Joram
Jorim	Uzziah
Eliezer	Jotham
Joshua	Ahaz
Er	Hezekiah
Elmadam	Manasseh
Cosam	Amos
Addi	Josiah
Melchi	Jechoniah
Neri	

Shealtiel	Salathiel
Zerubbabel_____	Zerubbabel
Rhesa, Joanan, Joda, Josech,	Abiud
Semein, Mattathias,	
Maath, Naggai, Esli, Nahum,	Eliakim
Amos	
Mattathias	Azor
Joseph	Zadok
Jannai	Achim
Melchi	Eliud
Levi	Eleazar
Matthat	Matthan
Heli	Jacob
Joseph _____	Joseph, *husband of Mary*

MATTHEW   Okay, everyone. We've got a task to do, so let's do it quickly. As you know, we have been charged by our leaders to straighten out the genealogy of our Lord Jesus Christ. I agree with them because we can't have two different *(looking at Luke)* genealogies of Jesus in the Bible! That would be too confusing for members of the church. *(He points to the chart on the wall.)* I have done some homework before our meeting and have written down the two genealogies side by side here—my community's and Luke's. I have matched up the names that we have in common. Now, all we need to do is to agree on the rest. Any suggestions?

LUKE   Well, Matthew, since your genealogy started only with Abraham, and mine goes all the way back to Adam, why don't we just add the section from Adam to Abraham to the final list? That's simple enough. Do we all agree?

MATTHEW   No, that would mess up the numbers.

JOHN   Numbers?

MATTHEW   You see, in my genealogy, there are fourteen generations from Abraham to David, fourteen generations from David to the exile in Babylon, and fourteen generations from Babylon to Joseph.

MARK   I know the four corners of the world, the five books of Moses, the seventh day as the Sabbath, and the twelve tribes of Israel. What's fourteen for?

MATTHEW   The numerical values of the three Hebrew letters in the name David—D, W, and D—add up to fourteen.

LUKE   Why should we care about that?

MATTHEW   Because King David is essential for us to understand the royal bloodline of Jesus. If you add this whole bunch of names, that would destroy the symbolism of the genealogy.

LUKE   Symbolism! I thought accuracy is what we're after.

MATTHEW   There is no accuracy to speak of. We don't really know who begot whom, do we?

LUKE   But...

MATTHEW   Can you prove that all these names you have of those who came after Zerubbabel in your list are accurate? I have never heard of these people.

LUKE   They were names passed down from our elders.

MATTHEW   Let's be real about this. I can't prove that these names on my list were real, either. But that's not the point.

MARK   I don't see the point of having a genealogy of Jesus in the Bible at all.

JOHN   I agree with Mark. Have you ever thought about why we are tracing Jesus' genealogy through Joseph's ancestry? He's not even the biological father of Jesus.

MATTHEW   That's not very helpful, John.

JOHN	All I am asking is, Who is the father of Jesus?
LUKE	God.
JOHN	Right. The whole purpose of the gospel is to show the divinity of Jesus. So having a human genealogy is antithetical to our whole purpose.
LUKE	Excuse me. But Jesus is also human. That's what Jesus was trying to show us on earth—our true humanity.
MARK	If we were to do a genealogy at all, shouldn't we be tracing Mary's bloodline?
MATTHEW	Again, accuracy isn't the point here.
LUKE	What is the point?
MATTHEW	The point is, What do we want to say to future generations that read the Bible? What message do we want to give them when they read the genealogy of our Lord Jesus Christ?
JOHN	Does anybody really read the genealogy in the Bible?
MATTHEW	Make a joke of it if you want. But every word we put in the Bible will send a message to future readers because they will investigate each word, each sentence. So I will ask the question again: What do we want to say to future generations with our genealogy?
MARK	That we are sexist?
LUKE	And classist.
MATTHEW	I included women in my genealogy, didn't I? See?— Tamar, Rahab, and Ruth, all poor women at that.
LUKE	Were there any rich women in those days?
MATTHEW	You don't even have women on your list!
LUKE	Okay, I agree that we should include women on our list. And I would agree with you that David should

be on the list along with Abraham and the patriarchs. But all these kings! Don't you think that's a little too much?

MATTHEW   Calling Jesus a king is not classist. He *is* the Messiah.

LUKE   Jesus' messiahship is not about ruling like an earthly king; he came to restore our humanity. That's why we have to trace him back to Adam, the first human being.

MATTHEW   You do know that in my Christmas story, I had the kings from the Orient, who were not Jewish, coming to worship our Lord Jesus. Jesus is the king for all nations.

LUKE   Jesus came to be with the poor, the helpless, the outcast. That's why the angels announced the birth of Jesus to the shepherds first in my book. Jesus did not come to make your upper-middle-class community happy.

MATTHEW   How on earth are the poor going to get anywhere if the rich do not start giving? The kingship of Jesus would challenge them to let go of their power and wealth. Can't you see we are really talking about the same thing?

LUKE   No, we are not. The rich will never willingly give up their power. That's why Jesus died on the cross to expose how they abused their power.

JOHN   In the beginning was the Word, and the Word was with God, and the Word was God.

MATTHEW   Please don't do that now, John.

JOHN   Isn't that enough of a statement about where Jesus came from?

MATTHEW   No, it's important for our people, especially those who were Jewish, to understand that Jesus was and is the Messiah for them. That is our heritage; we can't forget that.

JOHN   Jesus said, "I am the way, and the truth, and the life."

MATTHEW   Let's not go there, John. That's too fluffy for us practical folks.

MARK   Stop! Stop! Why do we have to write down everything and explain it to death? Why can't we just tell the simple story of Jesus? What he did? What he said? Why can't we trust future generations to figure out what it means to them?

MATTHEW   But your story of Jesus is so brief that it has many dangers for misinterpretations.

LUKE   Yes. Your story was so vague that you didn't even have the resurrection of Jesus told. Where is the good news?

MATTHEW   We had to force you to add the resurrection of our Lord to the end of your book!

MARK   In our community, we have to be very careful what we say and what we write down. If the government got a hold of it, we could be persecuted. So, I'd say, the less we say, the better.

MATTHEW   Mark, Christianity is now an accepted religion in most parts of the world. There is no need to tiptoe around any more. We can say what we mean.

MARK   But that's the problem: You say what you mean, and call *that* the truth according to your community. And you, Luke, say what you mean and call *that* the ultimate truth. And the two truths are different. Then what is the truth? Look at us now. We might not be persecuted for being Christians, but we are persecuting one another for having the wrong version of the story of Jesus.

JOHN   Truly, truly I say to you. The hour is coming when you will worship God neither in Jerusalem nor at the well of Jacob, but will worship God in spirit and truth.

MATTHEW   And what does that mean?

JOHN   You do know the story about Jesus meeting the Samaritan woman at the well?

MATTHEW   No, John. Only your community had that story. We never heard of it.

JOHN   That doesn't mean it didn't happen.

LUKE   I happen to like that story—Jesus talking to a non-Jew, and a woman at that.

MARK   Why don't we hear what John is trying to say instead of taking sides?

JOHN   In those days, the Jews said that God was in Jerusalem. The Samaritans said that God was at the well of Jacob. Jesus said that God is a living God and is not bounded by our temporal and spatial assumptions.

MATTHEW   So...

JOHN   No doubt the experience of God through the culture of the Jews was real. And the revelation of God through the culture of the Samaritans was also real. But God is more than that.

LUKE   And...

MARK   All our different versions of the story of Jesus are true and real according to our communities. But each version by itself is somewhat exclusive and incomplete, showing only one dimension of Christ.

LUKE   Are you saying that having our diverse versions of the story of Jesus is good?

MARK   Yes. We have to read these different stories in the spirit of discovering the greater truth—the living Christ who is greater than all four versions of the stories combined. Christ is more than that.

MATTHEW   And that's how Jesus can be a king to us.

LUKE	And a servant and liberator to us.
JOHN	And Jesus is divine.
LUKE	And human.
MARK	A mystery.
JOHN	And much more than that.
MATTHEW	*(Pause.)* What are we going to do now?
MARK	Why don't we leave the scriptures as they are, with all the discrepancies?
MATTHEW	Then how will the future generations discern the truth?
MARK	Like we just did. If we create one unified gospel story, we are not being true to who Christ was to each of our communities.
LUKE	By putting our different stories side by side in the Bible, we are saying to future generations that Christ is not static, like a written story on a page fixed in time and space.
JOHN	We are saying that Christ is above and beyond each one of these communities' stories of God.
MARK	And in their struggle to understand the discrepancies of the stories, people of each culture and generation will discover who Christ will be for them in their own contexts and not just according to Mark.
MATTHEW	Or Matthew.
LUKE	Or Luke.
JOHN	Or John.
MATTHEW	*(Pause.)* Well, good Christian folks, I believe our job is done. Let's go and tell the rest what we have decided.
	The End.

Of course, this was a fictional account of how it came to be that there were four different stories of the gospel in the Bible. Nevertheless, I believe that the dialogue captured some of the flavors of what might have gone on in that church council when they decided which texts should be included in the Bible. The early church leaders who put together the collection of writings in the Bible knew that the gospel has to be incarnated through a unique cultural expression in order for it to be real. In that sense, Jesus was born into a Jewish family. At an early age, he might have been in exile with his parents in Egypt, and then later settled in Galilee, a diverse border town in which intermingling of Jews and Gentiles was a part of daily life.[1] He exercised his ministry mainly in a Jewish community under the occupation of the Romans. In this specific context, Jesus revealed the truth about God to us through his words and actions.

Subsequently, as the gospels were received and experienced by more and more people, and when, eventually, the majority of the believers were no longer Jewish, the gospels were remembered, reexperienced, and written down differently according to different cultural contexts. The early church leaders knew that if they made any one of these versions of the story of Jesus the absolute one, they would, in effect, fix Jesus in a specific time and context. Then future generations would not be reading about the living Christ, but about a Jesus who acted once upon a time as remembered by a particular community. The record of the life and ministry of Christ would be in danger of becoming obsolete to future generations living in a changing world with new experiences and new contexts.

The early church leaders decided on a messy and puzzling way to keep the gospel alive for each generation that reads the Bible. They carefully selected four versions of the story of Jesus and put them side by side in one book and called them all true according to the four different contexts. This book, with its diversity, would challenge future generations to struggle and to dialogue with its inconsistency. This book, with its multicontextual milieu, would keep future generations from being idolatrous in claiming there is

---

[1]For a full exposition of the Galilean context in Jesus' time, see Virgilio Elizodo, *Galilean Journey* (New York: Orbis Books, 2000), 49–66.

only one way to believe—one way to relate to God through one specific cultural perception of Christ. The greater truth is somewhere in there if we read all the gospels together—not just one line, not just one story, not just two, but all of them. The goal is to capture that dynamic living relationship with Christ now in our own context, and not just slavishly model a copy of how one community or person had related to God through Jesus "once upon a time." We are more faithful if we hold the tension of these inconsistencies together for the purpose of finding that greater consistent truth about who Christ is as a living being who is still interacting with us now.

At the heart of our faith—the gospel stories—the tension of pluralism is maintained and held together in one book. At the center of our faith is where the crossing of different cultures occurred and is documented. The Bible has provided crossings in which we are invited to enter and explore and be challenged and affirmed, be puzzled and yet discover new ways of connecting with God through the living Christ. Each time we read a biblical text, we enter into the crossing of cultures embedded in the text, the cultural context of the different groups and persons in the story, the cultural context of the writer. And more importantly, the Bible invites us to bring our own cultural context to the crossings, challenging us to struggle and lift ourselves out of the static, fixed-in-time version of the revelation of God, so that we can encounter God anew in the crossing.

At my ordination to be a deacon in the Episcopal Church in 1984, I made a solemn declaration that "I do believe the Holy Scriptures of the Old and New Testaments to be the Word of God, and to contain all things necessary to salvation."[2]

As I said these words, I remembered my senior advisor in seminary telling me to just read the Bible, from beginning to end, as the principle way of preparing for my ordination examination. I remembered spending two months reading passages from the Bible that I didn't like, texts in which I had no idea what was meant, lines of scripture that confirmed my beliefs, and stories that challenged my deeply held values. All these words, sentences, paragraphs, stories, dreams, visions, characters with questionable

---

[2]*Book of Common Prayer*, 526.

morals, powerful characters in need of redemption, and lowly characters being lifted up were part of God's story in relating to humanity. All of it—"the Holy Scriptures of the Old and New Testaments," with its many discrepancies and inconsistencies among the different books and sometimes within the same book—contains "all things necessary to salvation." The Bible does not give an easy way out by giving us an absolute answer to every question that we have about life. The Bible provides us with crossings. The willingness to enter into the crossings and struggle with the diversity and discrepancies is a part of what is necessary for salvation. In that struggle, we discover anew who the living God is, how Christ challenges us to work for justice and mercy, and how the Holy Spirit inspires and connects us in spite of our differences, but still insists on forming us into one community of God.

Suggested Exercises

1. Rehearse the play in this chapter with four readers/actors. Present the play in a class. Afterward, invite the class to discuss the following questions:

    a. What did you learn in this play about the Bible and diversity?

    b. What might be a more faithful way to read the Bible as a community?

2. Invite a group of people with diverse backgrounds to study scriptures together using the Community Bible Study as described in my first book, *The Wolf Shall Dwell with the Lamb*.[3] In this kind of approach, we invite participants to listen and connect with the biblical text from their own perspectives and then share their insights. When the makeup of the group is diverse, the resulting sharing is enriched by the different contexts that the participants have brought with them to the community.

3. When studying a biblical text that has references to other similar texts in the Bible (especially among the gospels), read those texts together and invite the community to explore these questions:

---

[3]See Eric H. F. Law, *The Wolf Shall Dwell with the Lamb* (St. Louis: Chalice Press, 1993), 121–31.

a. Why were there differences among the texts?
b. What were the different contexts from which these texts emerged? Can you speculate what kind of communities and issues these different texts were trying address?
c. How were these contexts similar to or different from your own context?
d. What does this text say to you now?

4. Start a Community Bible Study group during the week and study the biblical texts that you will be using for your sermon on the upcoming Sunday. Make sure the makeup of the group is diverse in gender, age, economic status, education, race, and ethnicity, representing members of your community. Do not make yourself into an expert even though the participants might want you to tell them what the text means, but rather be only one voice, one context among many in the group. Most importantly, listen to the participants—their connections with the text, their relationships with God, their stories and yearnings. In preparing the final version of the sermon, keep the different contexts and stories in mind.

Chapter 3

Elephants at the Crossings

Five blind persons encounter an elephant. In their usual manner, they use their hands to touch and feel this unknown creature in order to learn what it is like.

One says, "I know what an elephant is like. It is like a great big barrel suspended in the air."

Another person says, "No, you're wrong; the elephant is like a big tree trunk."

"No," the third person argues, "The elephant is like a fan made with leather."

"No, the elephant is nothing like that. It's like a rope," says a fourth person.

And the fifth person says, "You are all wrong. The elephant is like a snake."

If the five blind persons continue to argue over who is right, they will never discover what a real elephant in its entirety is like. The only way they can know the whole elephant is to stop arguing and listen to one another and be puzzled by the differences. In that puzzlement, they might connect the different pieces of the puzzle that they each had. If they are successful in putting their different perspectives together, they might be able to more fully describe an elephant—the rope is actually the tail, the tree trunks are legs, the barrel is the body, the snake is the nose, and the fans are the ears.

This parable has been told for centuries in many cultures. I learned it when I was in grade school. There is a very old Chinese saying that captures this parable in four words: "blind persons touching elephant," which is a quick way of saying, "Don't be so quick to say you're right; the event is often much bigger than your perspective." But like most parables, there are many ways to interpret it and to connect with it. I suppose that's why Jesus used parables time and again to describe what he called "the kingdom of God." In my Christian life, I have found myself using, again and again, many Chinese parables that I learned when I was young to illustrate different points in my sermons. Using this parable as a springboard, I will offer a few interpretations in describing how we are to communicate the gospel in a diverse environment.

Interpretation 1

God is like the elephant in this parable. The Bible, with its diversity, gives us different points of contact with God. Each book, story, character, event, poem, letter, dream, and vision is like one of the blind persons in the parable: in contact with the Divine, but not able to fully describe the wholeness of God. Sometimes when I read a biblical text and make an instant connection with it, I think, "That really helps me understand my situation." This is because I might share a similar context with this particular biblical text. Very often I have found myself referring to these "favorite" texts in my teaching and preaching.

However, most of the time when I read an unfamiliar text in the Bible, my immediate reaction might be, "This makes no sense." This is because the context of the passage might be very different from my own. It is like a blind person holding onto the elephant's tail and being puzzled by the description of the elephant by another person touching the elephant's ear. When that happens, instead of dismissing or ignoring that text, I must acquire a sense of healthy puzzlement. The Bible is supposed to puzzle each of us with its diversity because it is not a book that was written specifically for me. It is meant to connect with many different people with diverse contexts. In the puzzlement, we are challenged not to simply take one text or line of the Bible and call that the whole truth for all people and all time just because that text happens to connect with us. We are called to struggle with the different stories and their different contexts and discover how the living God interacts, inspires, and challenges each one of these contexts differently. These contexts, in which the revelation of God occurred, may or may not be the same as our own contexts. Nevertheless, they were an authentic connection with the Divine. If we are to seek God in the wider context beyond our own, we must learn to appreciate and learn from this diversity of connection with the scripture. Our task in reading the Bible is twofold:

1. As we read the Bible, we may readily make connections with certain stories, characters, and events. We may be drawn to those biblical stories, characters, and events because they connect with our personal experiences and community life. We interpret the text by correlating our experiences with the situations described in the biblical story—the relationships between the characters and with God. In making the correlation, we can make contact with God.[1] In finding the similarity between our story and the biblical story, we are informed by God in what we are called to do. However, we need to be humble about our interpretation by recognizing that ours is but one of many ways to make contact with God, like one of the blind persons touching only a small part of the elephant.

2. As we read the Bible, we must also be open to the possibility of being puzzled by stories, characters, and events that might be very different from our own contexts and experiences. We struggle with these "foreign" stories and experiences while affirming that they were also part of the revelation of God, even though we may not readily connect with them. In the struggle, we are challenged to see the greater vision of God. That is, the elephant is bigger than what I can discern with just my two hands. Therefore, when reading the Bible with others, especially with those from a different cultural context, do not be surprised by how others relate to the same text by arriving at different, and sometimes opposite, interpretations. Instead, be puzzled by this difference, and resist the temptation to debate or defend your perspectives. Listen

---

[1]For a fuller description of this method, see Justo L. Gonzalez and Catherine G. Gonzalez, *The Liberating Pulpit* (Nashville: Abingdon Press, 1994), 66–95.

to the others, and attempt to make connections across the differences. Maybe, in the process, you and the others can describe God—the elephant—more faithfully together.

Interpretation 2

Living in a diverse, pluralistic world, we will encounter people with different connections, experiences, and relationships with God—like the five persons having different contacts with the elephant. This is because God chooses to connect with different communities and persons in different manners, according to their cultures and situations. We are called to witness and share how God has connected with us in the most authentic way according to our own experiences and contexts. But we must also know that there are other ways through which God has connected with persons and communities with different experiences and contexts than our own.

A mainline denomination hired a missioner to develop a new church in a specific neighborhood with a specific economic and language group. This was all planned down to the last detail, with exhaustive studies of the population in that neighborhood. The missioner, who had the same language skills and ethnicity as the majority of this community, used the latest techniques in new church development, and within two years the church grew to two hundred Sunday attendees. Most of the members of this church were new Christians. The pastor used worship styles and biblical texts that connected with these folks, and sure enough, they connected with God in that way and joined the church community. But because of the language and theological specificity of this new community, they had little contact with the rest of the member churches of their denomination, and the denomination did not make any effort to invite this new community to encounter the diverse membership of the church denomination. As a result, when the denomination voted on a controversial issue, resulting in a decision that did not agree with the narrow theology of the members of this new community, the new community broke away and left the denomination, becoming further isolated from the rest of the wider and diverse Christian community.

With the hard work of the missioner, these new Christians no doubt had a life-changing experience of the revelation of God through Christ. In their minds, their way of knowing God must be the only way. However, when the broader church did not continue to teach them about the greatness of God, they settled into a very narrow understanding of God. They believed that their version of the elephant was the whole elephant. The whole church community (not only the ministers!) has a responsibility to continue to teach each new Christian that his or her experience of the Divine is but one way; each is like one of the five blind persons having only a limited, incomplete contact with the elephant. We must teach them the discipline of listening to one another's experiences of the revelation of God with a healthy puzzlement or a helpful curiosity, with the hope of gaining a greater, fuller understanding of God. We must teach them to reach across their differences to make connections, because it is through these connections that we are better able to see a greater vision of God.

This is why Jesus said, "Love your enemies" and "God makes God's sun rise on the evil and on the good, and sends rain on the righteous and on the unrighteous." When we claim that our contact with God is the only way, the only conclusion we can make about others who have had another type of contact with God is that they are our enemies or the evil ones. Jesus teaches us that our God is greater than what an individual or group thinks. The people that you think are your enemies are also children of God. Jesus also commands us to pray for our enemies. He urges us to reach across our differences and make connection through prayers.

When the blind persons decide to stop arguing and instead begin to listen to one another and eventually make connections with the different parts that they know, they have a better chance of learning the truth about the whole elephant. When I stop insisting that my experience of God is the only valid way, and when I am willing to struggle to make connection with those who have a different experience of God, we all have a greater opportunity to see a fuller vision of God.

Interpretation 3

In the 1980s, I attended many anti-racism training and diversity workshops. A recurring, frustrating experience for me was having to listen to people arguing over whose definition of racism was more correct. Sometimes in these diversity workshops, I heard people arguing over whose pain was greater. These were frustrating experiences, because by arguing with one another about whose perspectives were more real, valid, or correct, we were letting these "isms" continue to have their power over us—to divide us.

The elephant in the parable could be an issue such as racism, sexism, homophobia, ableism, ageism, classism, and so forth. Those of us whose lives have been affected by these "isms" are like the blind persons, having only our own limited contact with the larger issue. Some of us might have benefited from these "isms." Some of us were hurt and diminished and devalued by them. Nevertheless, we will not be effective in dismantling these "isms" if we continue to argue about whose experiences were more painful or valid and whose definitions of them are more correct. We have to work together by listening to one another's versions and experiences of these "isms." When we are able to make connections through one another's offerings, we begin to see a fuller description of these creatures, these principalities, and these powers. When we can name these principalities and powers together, we can work together to dismantle them.

In a typical interracial dialogue program, I usually utilize a tool called Photolanguage[2] as the centerpiece of a five-session program. By the third session, participants have already practiced speaking responsibly and listening empathetically, and they have developed trust among themselves. Participants in this session are invited to look at a set of forty-eight photographs and chose two photos to answer these questions:

1.   What is racism for me?
2.   How has racism affected my life?

The participants are then invited to share, using the photos that they have selected. In this kind of session, we do not begin by presenting any specific definition of racism—doing so would leave open the door for a possible debate if there are people there

---

[2]The Photolanguage that I have developed is called "Interactions," which consists of 48 black-and-white photographs. For a full description of the process and its origin, see Eric H. F. Law, *The Wolf Shall Dwell with the Lamb* (St. Louis: Chalice Press, 1993), 94, 115–19.

who disagree with it. Instead of beginning with a narrowing process of discussion definition, we begin by inviting participants to share their different experiences of racism, making sure that there is no debate or judgment. In one dialogue process that I facilitated in an interracial group from a southern state in the United States, I had the privilege of listening to African Americans who were the descendants of slaves and European Americans who were descendants of slave owners sitting in a circle sharing and listening to how racism as expressed in the institution of slavery affected their lives. At the end of the sharing time, there were tears and embraces. I saw a glimpse of the possibility of reconciliation, and there were discussions on how to work together to dismantle racism—black and white together. When the blind persons are able to work together to more fully describe the elephant, they work together to tame it rather than continuing to be trampled by it.

Interpretation 4

Over the years, as I have delivered numerous workshops and presentations on multicultural ministry and building inclusive community, I have encountered two recurring attitudes toward diversity. On the surface, one seems to be in support of diversity and "tolerance," and the other against it. But on further reflection, either one is but a reaction against the other. They don't really support diversity, because both attitudes discourage people from making connections. At one extreme is what I call the "absolutist" camp. To them, there is only one set of universal absolute truths, and anyone who does not conform to it is wrong. If they had been in control in the formation of the Christian Scriptures, they would have been tempted to reconcile all the differences and create a uniform universal text of the gospel story that would claim to have direct application to all cultures across all time and space. An "absolutist" blind person would insist that his or her version of the elephant is universal.

At the other extreme is what I called the "relativist" camp. They would say that since the world is so diverse, no absolute exists anymore. No one cultural group can judge another because the standards for right and wrong are so different among the different cultures. And, therefore, people can do what they want and believe what they want. Any talk of an absolute or a standard is irrelevant and oppressive to a free-thinking society. If the "relativist" group had been around when the Christian Scriptures had been put together, they would have been tempted not to have *one* sacred book with *the* story at all. They would have allowed all the little books to continue to have their lives in different communities and not to say anything about right or wrong, nor to judge any one of them as orthodoxy or heresy. A "relativist" blind person would say that everyone is entitled to his or her version of the elephant. There is no right or wrong elephant.

Neither extreme allows for making interpersonal connection or dialogue across differences and, therefore, neither has room for discovering the greater truth. On the "absolutist" side, you either agree with them or you do not. If you agree, they will have dealings with you; if you don't, they don't need to deal with you anymore. On the "relativist" side, you don't need to agree with them, nor do they need to deal with you, either; everyone can just do his or her own thing.

The Bible situates itself somewhere in between these two extremes. To the "absolutist," the Bible says there are particularities and uniqueness in how God, through Christ, responded to different diverse communities; just read the different stories and memories of the same event in Jesus' life. In other words, there are different parts of the elephant. To the "relativist," the Bible says that there is a universal standard to how God has challenged and judged everyone and every community in this diverse world. There are basic convictions that Christians commit themselves to that are applicable to all people in different contexts. Read about how God has challenged and affirmed individuals and communities through Christ's absolute commitment to compassion and justice for all people in the different stories you have found in the Bible. In other words, there is the whole elephant, not just the parts.

> *One of them, a lawyer, asked [Jesus] a question to test him. "Teacher, which commandment in the law is the greatest?" He said to him, "'You shall love the Lord your God with all your heart, and with all your soul, and with all your mind.' This is the greatest and first commandment. And a second is like it: 'You*

shall love your neighbor as yourself.' On these two commandments hang all the law and the prophets." (Mt. 22:35–40)

As recorded in the Christian Scriptures, the religious leaders of Jesus' time seemed to be of the "absolutist" camp. There were the absolute standards of the Law, and one had to follow it or one would be excluded. The reason that this question from a lawyer was a test for Jesus was that, time and again, Jesus broke the laws that they considered absolute. For example, Jesus ate with sinners, tax collectors, and people who were considered unclean; Jesus also healed people during the Sabbath. Jesus broke the law in order to show God's love and conviction for justice to the people whom he encountered. Jesus came across to the religious leaders of his time as someone who had no regard for the law. To them, Jesus was a "relativist" type of teacher. They were concerned that if Jesus continued to break the rules, and because he had all these followers, their religious institution as they knew it might end.

The answer Jesus gave implied that even though they might think that he was a "relativist" type of teacher, there was a standard to what he did. Even though the Law came from God to the Israelites through Moses, Jesus was saying that the Law was not the full expression of God's will for all people. Many standards of the Law were too specific to one particular cultural group, and if applied blindly to every situation without taking the local contexts into consideration, the specifics of the Law could be oppressive to some members of the community, especially those who were poor and powerless. But Jesus did not say that everything was relative. Jesus put forth the great commandments as the central primary agreement that we must have in order to live like him.

Jesus came not to abolish the Law but to fulfill it. Jesus fulfilled the Law by pointing to the living God who gave us the Law to start out with. Jesus fulfilled the Law by inviting us to let go of the static expression of God's actions in a particular time and place, and instead to focus on the living God who interacts with individual persons and communities differently according to the different contexts *now*. Jesus invites us to move from the legalistic boundaries of who is in and who is out and to travel toward the center, which is the living God who demands our love with all our hearts, souls, minds, and strengths *now*. Jesus invites us to reach toward the center that connects all of us by loving our neighbors as ourselves. In making the connections, we might gain a fuller vision of God and what God demands of us and, therefore, know how to love God with all our being. In other words, Jesus invites us to focus on the wholeness of the elephant—the living God— the being through which our different parts can connect.

I was at a craft show, and a woman was selling bracelets with the initials: WWJD. I innocently asked her, "What does that stand for?"

She said, "What would Jesus do?"

Some of us might think that this is corny. But do not dismiss this idea so quickly. In a world where everything is changing at a quicker pace than we would like; in a world where neighborhoods can have a complete transfusion of new populations with different cultures and backgrounds in only a few years; in a world where there does not seem to be any solid ground of values to stand on; in a world where fragmented groups, in their uncertainty, are busy drawing boundaries of separation, we need to remember WWJD every day, if not every second, of our lives. This is because what worked yesterday might not work today. What was right yesterday might be wrong today. We can no longer rely on absolutes, and yet we cannot live without some kind of standard.

Jesus lived in a space where he seemed to defy the absolute rules, and yet there is a definitive ethic to what he did. Jesus did not rely on sets of rules to determine what he would do. To us, he seemed to decide what to do on the spot; all the while, we are still asking him to tell us what the rules are. We might demand in our heart, "Tell me what to do so I don't have to think every time." But Jesus' way requires us to think every time about every situation and about every relationship. The way Jesus heard, saw, felt, and acted in the world according to the great commandments seemed to be so hard to comprehend that he had to explain it again and again in different ways, even to his closest disciples— sometimes very directly, sometimes using parables. The long list of parables of the kingdom of God was his attempt to explain this divine thing that he was trying to describe. We are still struggling with the meaning of these stories, and we still hear the echoing refrain, "Let those who have ears, hear."

Jesus tried to describe the elephant to the people around him and to us, but we continue to be like the blind persons holding onto our own small parts and refusing to reach across and connect with others. Jesus yearned to pull us from our separateness and called us to the crossings to struggle and make connections with our differences. He finally showed us how to do this through his death and resurrection. The ultimate puzzle he presented to us was the connection between something so seemingly unredeemable as dying on the cross, and the glorious resurrection. Jesus' invitation to make this connection between death and new life was his final triumph, showing us who God was and is for all time. Jesus invites us to follow him; to see, listen, feel, and act in the world as he did so that we can experience that divine thing that he was trying to tell us. His challenge for us and for the church to follow his life pattern is a lifelong task for every Christian and for the church. Jesus' willingness to take up the cross is his invitation to us to enter the crossings of differences with courage and the assurance of God's love. Jesus' resurrection gives us hope that by making connections with one another—loving one another as we love ourselves even though we disagree with one another—we will find the truth and new life together.

Suggested Exercises

1. Read a biblical story and meditate on how each character in the story experienced the event described. Write a monologue for each character describing his or her point of view. Explore how the different characters connect with one another. Explore how the idea and concept of God is exposed more fully through the connections that these characters make with one another. Construct a sermon by taking different characters' perspectives and end by answering the question, How did God/Christ challenge the different characters differently in the story, and how does God challenge those of us who have different backgrounds and experiences?

2. Read a biblical story aloud, and invite the listeners to imagine that they each are one of the characters in the story. Invite them to consider how that character sees, hears, and feels in the story. Have a period of silence after the reading for them to finish their imagining. Invite them to share their insights

and how their meditation helps them understand how God acts in people's lives.

3. Invite individuals in your group to describe a favorite biblical text and the reasons why it is so meaningful. After participants have shared, invite them to reflect on what they have heard from one another and what they have learned about the Bible and God that day.

4. Take a contemporary issue and invite participants who are from different sides of the issue to come and share their perspectives. Make sure they share in a respectful manner by first presenting the "Respectful Communication Guidelines" or "Dialogue Ground Rules,"[3] and invite them to uphold them for the time they are together. Also, using the technique "Mutual Invitation"[4] will ensure that everyone is invited to share. You might want to use Photolanguage as a tool for facilitating a more in-depth, emotive sharing. After they have shared, invite participants to reflect on what they have heard and how, by listening, they can see a fuller picture of the issue. This might lead to the question, What should we as a community do about the issue, having heard the different perspectives?

---

[3]See Eric H. F. Law, *The Bush Was Blazing but Not Consumed* (St. Louis: Chalice Press, 1996), 86.

[4]See Law, *The Wolf Shall Dwell*, 79–88, 113–14.

Chapter 4

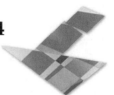

The Truth at the Crossings

"What is truth?" (Jn. 18:38a)

This was the question Pilate asked Jesus at the end of what seemed to be a frustrating interrogation. Pilate, who was not a Jew, was caught in an intercultural situation in which he could not understand the values and beliefs of the people who were demanding Jesus' death. He tried to avoid having to be the one to make this life-or-death decision by asking the crowd, "What accusation do you bring against this man?" (Jn. 18:29b). They answered, "If this man were not a criminal, we would not have handed him over to you" (Jn. 18:30). This answer did not give him the truth—as in actual facts or evidence—that he was looking for. Having no success in trying to get the crowd to judge Jesus according to their own law, Pilate went back to Jesus and posed this question: "Your own nation and the chief priests have handed you over to me. What have you done?" (Jn. 18:35). Again, Pilate was searching for the truth, looking for the proof of any criminal acts that Jesus might have committed.

Jesus answered him by talking about his kingdom, which is "not from this world." What he said must have been totally incomprehensible to Pilate. Perhaps out of frustration or maybe ridicule, "Pilate asked him, 'So you are a king?' Jesus answered, 'You say that I am a king. For this I was born, and for this I came into the world, to testify to the truth. Everyone who belongs to the truth listens to my voice'" (Jn. 18:37).

Then, Pilate asked the question, "What is truth?" for which he did not get an answer. One can interpret his question "What is truth?" as a sarcastic remark, because he knew that the truth, as in actual facts—what Jesus had done that deserved to be punished by death—had nothing to do with this situation, but politics and power had everything to do with it. Or perhaps Pilate was asking the question that we need to ask today: What is truth in a pluralistic world where there are different values held by different cultural groups to measure what the truth is for them? Or perhaps Pilate had no conceptual framework to understand what Jesus meant by "the truth," hence the question.

In a court of law in the United States, a person, before testifying, swears to tell the truth, the whole truth, and nothing but the truth. The concept of truth here is contrasted with a lie or information not based on observable, physical evidence. This is often how we use this term in our everyday English language. Perhaps this kind of truth was what Pilate was asking of the crowd and of Jesus. Searching for the factual truth often means judging and proving that someone might be lying. But measurable and observable factual truth is often interpreted politically to support one's theory of what is the truth. I call this "interpreted truth." Again, in a court of law, the lawyers on both sides have arranged the same facts in ways that support their different theories of what actually happened—the truth. The jury is asked to determine which interpreted truth is correct. The one presenting his or her version of the interpreted truth is more interested in winning than in finding out what really happened, because winning means becoming the one who defines the truth, which then may be recorded and become part of history. Finding the truth by debating whose interpreted truth is correct is a political maneuver, in which the more powerful group, using what they consider to be factual and scientific proof to back up their claims, will eventually take control and define the truth for the others.

There is also what I call "experienced truth," which is the truth as remembered by a group or a person. Experienced truth, like interpreted truth, is by nature subjective. It is the truth as interpreted through the lens of the person's or group's cultural framework and worldview. For example, in the experience of childbirth, the factual truth is that a mother gave birth to a child who is a girl weighing 7.5 lbs. at 1:15 a.m. Those present were the doctor, a nurse, and the father. These are the factual truths. The experienced truth for the mother would be quite different from that of the father. The experienced truth of the doctor and of the nurse would be very different from that of the parents. The experienced truth of the child would also be very different from that of the rest of the people in the same room in the same event. All the experienced truths as remembered by the different parties are all true according to their experiences. We cannot really say which one is more true than the others. Alan Jones, in his book *Living the Truth,* says, "What you think is the truth depends on what you believe. What you think is the truth depends on who you think you are."[1]

In a pluralistic society, if we are to value each group's experienced truth, and if these truths are different, how do we determine what is the truth? Whose truth are we talking about? How do we make ethical decisions? Does that make everything relative? If each party claims their truth is *the* truth, how do we proceed from this crossing of different truths?

Often, like lawyers in a court, the different groups engage one another in a political process—let's determine who has more power first, and then the powerful ones' experienced truth will become the normative truth. The powerful lay claim to their experience as the ultimate truth while the powerless' experiences are often ignored, put down, and even disproved. In that sense, what is accepted as the truth in a society might not be *the* truth of what actually happened at all. It might be merely the truth as experienced and defined by the historically dominant group of the society. As an example, for many years in U.S. history books, we were taught that Columbus discovered America. But for the Native Americans, that event was the beginning of the invasion by Europeans, resulting in the loss of their land, identity, and livelihood. The experienced truth of the Native Americans was ignored, not taught in our school, and left out of our history books because the powerful defined and controlled what they claimed to be the truth. Furthermore, they used their power and influence to propagate their version of the truth throughout the system.

---

[1] Alan Jones, *Living the Truth* (Cambridge, Mass.: Cowley Publications, 2000), 40.

The truth to which Jesus testified is a truth of a different order. It is not factual, interpreted, or experienced truth. How do we begin to grasp this concept and not stumble, like Pilate?

After seeing a good play or movie, we have often heard people say, "Now, that was good because there was some truth to that movie." We know that a play or a movie is mostly fictional—someone wrote the script; actors were employed to play different roles; the director directed it. So how can any truth, as in "facts," be told through such a medium? Obviously, when we use the word *truth* in this context, we are taking about a different order of truth. We are naming a pattern of interactions that exemplifies something very significant and important to life, and we are calling that the truth. Perhaps this is the kind of truth that Jesus was testifying to.

The concept of truth in both the gospel of John and Paul's writing is much closer to the meaning of the word *truth* in the Hebrew Scripture. The word *truth* corresponds frequently with a Hebrew noun derived from a verb that means "to sustain," or "to support." This same word in the Hebrew Scriptures can be translated as steadiness, unchangeability, stability, soundness, faithfulness, constancy, truth, loyalty, or justice according to different contexts. In fact, in many translations of the Bible, this same word for "truth" is translated as "faithfulness."[2]

The concept of truth, with reference to God, seems to designate a quality of God's nature or will or pattern of action. The God of Israel was a God of the truth as opposed to a true god. And this quality of God, the truth, can be discerned by observing God's action. This truth is unchangeable, constant, loyal, and just. This truth about God is the reason why we can trust God. God's truth, as in faithfulness, is constantly with the oppressed even at the most devastating times in people's lives. This truth, as in steadfastness and loyalty, is still there even when the people rebel against God. If we are to speak the truth, we are to speak and act in accordance with God's nature.

> O LORD, who may abide in your tent?
> Who may dwell on your holy hill?

---

[2]See *The Interpreter's Dictionary of the Bible* (Nashville: Abingdon Press, 1962), 714.

Those who walk blamelessly, and do what is right,
    and speak the truth from their heart.

                                            (Ps. 15:1–2)

One of the patterns of God's actions that expresses this truth is God's consistent raising up of the lowly, empowering those whom society has defined as powerless, while challenging the powerful to let go of their power. The Song of Mary describes this pattern in the gospel of Luke. It is a prediction of the pattern of Jesus' ministry as a continuation of what God had been doing for Israel:

My soul magnifies the Lord,
    and my spirit rejoices in God my Savior,
for he has looked with favor on the lowliness of his servant.
    Surely, from now on all generations will call me blessed…
    [H]e has scattered the proud in the thoughts of their hearts.
He has brought down the powerful from their thrones,
    and lifted up the lowly;
he has filled the hungry with good things,
    and sent the rich away empty.

                                            (Lk. 1:46–48, 51b–53)

The Song of Mary describes a shift in power—the lowly being lifted up and the powerful being brought down. It reminds us of a pattern that God had put forth from the beginning of salvation history as recorded in the Hebrew Scriptures—shifts in power occur between Jacob and Esau, Joseph and his brothers, the Israelites and Pharaoh, and so forth. Jesus' ministry continued this pattern. A sampling of his sayings capture this pattern: The last shall be first, the first shall be last; blessed are the poor; woe to you who are rich; it is easier for a camel to go through the eye of a needle than for someone who is rich to enter the kingdom of God; and so forth. The truth to which Jesus was testifying is a pattern of actions that produces this powerful shift.

And a woman in the city, who was a sinner, having learned that
[Jesus] was eating in the Pharisee's house, brought an alabaster
jar of ointment. She stood behind him at his feet, weeping, and
began to bathe his feet with her tears and to dry them with her
hair. Then she continued kissing his feet and anointing them with

the ointment. Now when the Pharisee who had invited him saw it, he said to himself, "If this man were a prophet, he would have known who and what kind of woman this is who is touching him—that she is a sinner." Jesus spoke up and said to him, "Simon, I have something to say to you." "Teacher," he replied, "Speak." "A certain creditor had two debtors; one owed five hundred denarii, and the other fifty. When they could not pay, he canceled the debts for both of them. Now which of them will love him more?" Simon answered, "I suppose the one for whom he canceled the greater debt." And Jesus said to him, "You have judged rightly." Then turning toward the woman, he said to Simon, "Do you see this woman? I entered your house; you gave me no water for my feet, but she has bathed my feet with her tears and dried them with her hair. You gave me no kiss, but from the time I came in she has not stopped kissing my feet. You did not anoint my head with oil, but she has anointed my feet with ointment. Therefore, I tell you, her sins, which were many, have been forgiven; hence she has shown great love. But the one to whom little is forgiven, loves little." Then he said to her, "Your sins are forgiven." But those who were at the table with him begin to say among themselves, "Who is this who even forgives sins?" And he said to the woman, "Your faith has saved you; go in peace." (Lk. 7:37–50)

At the beginning of this story, Simon the Pharisee was the powerful one, as a host and as a respected member of the religious community at the time. The woman from the city was considered a sinner and had no political standing in either society or the religious community. She was probably considered unclean and an outcast to be ignored. The power perception among the players in this story was clear and simple, but simplistic. At the end of the story, the lowly woman was raised up as someone who had done more for Jesus than Simon. She was forgiven more; she was considered more faithful than Simon. The power shift occurred when Jesus told a story, putting forth a very conventional understanding of forgiving debts that Simon certainly could agree with and understand. Then Jesus switched the values by which we measure people's worth. Instead of measuring one's worth by one's status and privileges, Jesus emphasized the values of hospitality and forgiveness. By the action of the woman and her gratefulness for being forgiven, she was more than Simon, more powerful, more faithful, and more loving in God's eyes. Jesus affected the power shift with his presence, his words, and his actions. He testified to the truth.

As I reviewed my experience of the "presence of Christ" in my ministry, I began to discover this pattern as well. In many situations, the moment when I recognized the presence of the Divine—the moment of truth—was the moment when there was a shift in power. The formerly powerless were empowered, and the formerly powerful were letting go of their control; in this shift, there was, often for the first time, true honest communication and understanding, leading to possible reconciliation. The way of Christ facilitates this power shift, which is the process by which we can testify to the truth.

The pastor of Christ Church had retired. The denominational leader felt that this would be an opportunity to help the people of Christ Church to clarify their identity and mission before calling a new pastor. Hence, I was invited to spend a day consulting with the congregation. I brought along with me an observer, a trusted friend and colleague who would tell the truth about my role and the interactions among the congregation members. After some initial introductions, I presented the "Respectful Communication Guidelines,"[3] which is a standard piece I always do before I start any group. The guidelines were met with some resistance, especially from a few men in the room. By this time, I had made the observation that the majority of those present were women. Finally, after some discussion, the whole group agreed to uphold the guidelines. While we were taking a break, my observer came to me and said, "There seem to be three very powerful and vocal men in this room, and people are afraid to contradict them." I concurred with her observation.

Back when I was an inexperienced consultant, I would have sought to challenge these powerful men, because, as I had

---

[3]For a full description and usage of the "Respectful Communication Guidelines," see Eric H. F. Law, *The Bush Was Blazing but Not Consumed* (St. Louis: Chalice Press, 1996), 83–87.

interpreted the gospel then, my task was to raise up the lowly; that meant, according to my misinterpretation at the time, to bring down the powerful using my power to do so. Over the years I have learned that by focusing on the powerful few, I was actually reaffirming their power and influence and that my engagement with the powerful with my power would only serve to disempower the rest of the community members, who would then become powerless observers. Now I have learned that the way to proclaim the gospel—to testify to the truth—is not to engage the power personally, but to find ways for the rest of the community members to empower one another.

I continued with my agenda, which included a "Community Bible Study"[4] in which the participants were divided into small groups of six people, and each person in the group was invited to share his or her insight using "Mutual Invitation."[5] I knew that even with the Mutual Invitation process, these three men would still dominate the discussions. But since all three of them were in the same group, they could not dominate the other five groups in the room. I wanted the majority of the people in the room to have an empowered experience in the Bible study process.

Following that, the major part of the morning was devoted to an exercise called "Exploring the History of the Congregation."[6] In this exercise, I divided the participants into groups by the decade in which they became active at Christ Church. The three "powerful" men who joined the church in the 1960s were again confined to the same group. Even though they dominated that group's discussion, the other decades' groups were quite inclusive in the way they conducted their discussions; some groups even used the newly learned process of Mutual Invitation. We had a wonderful time as each decade's group reported—some reminisced on the good old days, and some surprised the others by reporting on secrets and treasures of the past.

---

[4]The full description of the "Community Bible Study" is in appendix C of Eric H. F. Law, *The Wolf Shall Dwell with the Lamb* (St. Louis: Chalice Press, 1993), 121–31.

[5]"Mutual Invitation" was first presented in my first book, Law, *The Wolf Shall Dwell*, 79–88. Over the years, this technique has become a principal tool for inclusive group process.

[6]See Eric H. F. Law, *Inclusion* (St. Louis: Chalice Press, 2000), 125–26.

After lunch, through an exercise called "Is Your Church Ministry Balanced?"[7] the participants joined three different groups according to their roles and individual interests:

Ministry *of* the Church

Ministry *in* the Church

Ministry *to* the Church.

Again, the three men chose the same group—Ministry *to* the Church. The task of this group was to explore the organization and leadership structure that supported the ministries *of* and *in* the church. The three groups did their work and then returned to report their findings.

After these exercises, I invited the participants to review all the reports, which were now posted on the wall. I asked if they could see any common themes, patterns, or myths that emerged out of these reports. During the break, my observer and I did the same process and discovered that consistently in every decade and in all three areas of ministries, the Women's Group was named as the key group that carried on the church's ministries. As they stared at these reports, they could not help but see what we saw. A few women in the group spoke with delight, "I knew that the Women's Group had always been there, but seeing it this way really makes me appreciate what women have done for this community." As we moved further into the discussion, we discovered that the founders of this church were all women. Contrary to what we had observed on the surface, which indicated to us that the three men were in charge, the women had been and were still the real leaders of the church all along.

The last hour was devoted to helping the congregation to discover their future ministry and identity. When the discussion began, I observed that the three men, for the first time, were silent. They became listeners while the rest of the group, mostly women, contributed and determined the future direction of their church. In the parking lot, my observer said to me with delight, "Did you see that? Did you see how the powerful few became quiet? I have never seen that happen before. That was magical."

---

[7]Ibid., 127–30.

A year later, I ran into some of the women from Christ Church at a church convention. They enthusiastically introduced me to their new pastor, who was a Native American. "We chose him to be our pastor," the women said proudly. "He was exactly the right person to help us grow and reach out to the neighborhood." The pastor then said to me, "I don't know what you did with the people in my church a year ago. They were so alive and still talking about that day when things started turning around."

What did I do? I later reflected on that experience. Together with my colleague and the people of this community, we created a crossing—the true encounter of people beyond the prescribed and assumed roles. The way we created this crossing was to facilitate a power shift. Instead of continuing the pattern of a few persons dominating while the majority let them, we created a "grace margin,"[8] in which everyone's input was welcome and listened to, where everyone participated. In the process, the seemingly powerful became silent. The seemingly powerless were empowered to speak, and they took the lead in the future direction of the church community. In the switching of power, the presence of Christ was made known. We experienced the Word at the crossing. We testified to the truth.

This is what I call the divine truth. Testifying to the divine truth means valuing the people around us as consistently as God has done. It means delivering the oppressed, raising up the lowly, and liberating the powerless exactly as God has done. It means challenging the powerful to let go and exposing their abuse of power as God has done. Testifying to the divine truth is using our bodies, minds, words, and actions as an extension of God's action and will in the world. It means transforming the world as God has done. It means patterning our lives according to God's pattern, so well exemplified by Jesus' ministry. It means seeing the truth as Jesus would see it, speaking the truth as Jesus would speak it, acting for the truth as Jesus would have acted for it. Jesus calls each one of us to continue this truth in our words and actions by following his way.

> *"If you continue in my word, you are truly my disciples; and you will know the truth, and the truth will make you free." (Jn. 8:31a–32)*

---

[8]"Grace margin" is a key concept for building an inclusive community I presented in *Inclusion*, 39–47.

There are a number of attributes about the divine truth that I would like to point out.

The divine truth challenged the truth as propagated by the historically dominant group.

[Jesus] sat down opposite the treasury, and watched the crowd putting money into the treasury. Many rich people put in large sums. A poor widow came and put in two small copper coins, which are worth a penny. Then he called his disciples and said to them, "Truly I tell you, this poor widow has put in more than all those who are contributing to the treasury. For all of them have contributed out of their abundance; but she out of her poverty has put in everything she had, all she had to live on." (Mk. 12:41–44)

The factual truth of this event was that a large sum of money was much more than two copper coins. The truth as concluded by the people watching this event was that the people who gave a large sum of money contributed more than the widow's two copper coins. The truth that Jesus saw was that the poor widow was giving, proportionally, much more than the rich people who gave large sums. Two copper coins were 100 percent of this widow's income, whereas the large sums that the rich people were giving might only have been a small percentage of their income. If you look at our churches' giving record in the way Jesus looked at that of the poor widow, you will also discover the same truth— that poor churches give proportionally much more than churches with members from higher income brackets. If we see the truth as Jesus sees it, do we value the voice of the churches that gave the most money or do we value the voice of the churches that give proportionally higher?

Jesus had a different way of assessing the truth. He looked not from the powerful people's perspective, but from a different angle with a different set of criteria that raised up the powerless. **Jesus' approach to revealing the truth begins with raising the self-esteem of the powerless.**

Paulo Freire, in his classic book *Pedagogy of the Oppressed*, speaks of the leader or teacher as the one who enables the powerless to see the real reality of their situation and not simply accept the incomplete reality imposed by the dominant group. In unveiling the reality through conscious articulation of their own experiences, the oppressed can then take action in transforming their situation. This process begins with empowering the powerless to articulate their experienced truth.

> Human existence cannot be silent, nor can it be nourished by false words, but only by true words, with which men and women transform the world...But while to say the true word—which is work, which is praxis—is to transform the world, saying the word is not the privilege of some few persons, but the right of everyone. Consequently, no one can say a true word alone—nor can she say it for another, in a prescriptive act which robs others of their words...Those who have been denied their primordial right to speak their word must first reclaim this right and prevent the continuation of this dehumanizing aggression.[9]

We don't have the whole truth unless we listen to stories of the powerless first.

"Where does that leave the powerful?" a participant in one of my workshops asked after I talked about how God raised up the powerless first. "I am willing to listen and to let go of control, but what comes after that? I am tired of going to antiracism workshops and being told that I am a racist and then not knowing what I should do next."

I told him that I had had similar experiences after attending antiracism and diversity workshops in the past. Challenging the powerful to let go of their power was only part of the process. We had to work on continuing the process so that no one was left feeling totally powerless, because I did not believe that this was what God wanted us to do. Then I said, "Jesus said, 'When you go to a wedding, don't sit at the honor seat.' But this does not mean you don't get to sit down and eat with the rest of the people in the party. It just means that you will sit at a different spot, intermingling with different folks. Jesus said, 'The first shall be last.' But that does not mean you are shut out of the action at all. It just means you still get to say what's on your mind after you have

[9]Paulo Freire, *Pedagogy of the Oppressed* (New York: Continuum, 1970), 69.

listened to the others first. It means you still get to do something after you have initially let go of your control."

To testify to the divine truth means inviting the powerful to listen while empowering the powerless to articulate their experiences and reality. But the process cannot stop here because if we leave it here, we are in danger of continuing the destructive cycle of domination because the formerly powerless, being in their empowered state, may become the oppressors. Instead, the process of truth-telling must continue, in which the formerly powerful, having listened to the reality as experienced by the powerless, can reflect and share their experienced truth in the context of the fuller description of the real reality. But the process must continue still, where the former speaker is then invited to listen again, and the former listener is invited to speak. It is in the cycle of dialogue that we can move deeper and deeper into—and reveal more and more of—the truth.[10]

> *"You have heard that it was said, 'You shall love your neighbor and hate your enemy.' But I say to you, Love your enemies and pray for those who persecute you, so that you may be children of your Father in heaven; for [God] makes [God's] sun rise on the evil and on the good, and sends rain on the righteous and on the unrighteous." (Mt. 5:43–45)*

The divine truth to which Jesus testified pushes us beyond our own experienced truth, whether we are powerful or powerless. He calls us to see the truth in a more global way, as God sees us and the world. Yes, God begins the truth-telling with the powerless, but God does not stop there. God challenges us to see the truth from all sides, including from those whom we consider our enemy. **The divine truth is a global truth.**

In South Africa, the postapartheid power shift finally happened in 1994. The people elected Nelson Mandela as their president. The formerly powerless were now speaking loudly, and the formerly powerful were at least standing still. What should the next step be? Archbishop Desmond Tutu, in his book

---

[10]For a fuller description of this process, what I have called the "Cycle of Gospel Living," see Law, *The Wolf Shall Dwell*, 71–78.

documenting the work of the Commission on Truth and Reconciliation, writes:

> [South Africa] rejected the two extremes and opted for a "third way," a compromise between the extreme of Nuremberg trails [in which we put the formerly powerful on trial for the purpose of punishing them for their criminal acts] and blanket amnesty or national amnesia. And that third way was granting amnesty to individuals in exchange for a full disclosure relating to the crime for which amnesty was being sought. It was a carrot of possible freedom in exchange for truth.[11]

The Commission set up meetings in which the experienced truths of both the victims and the victimizers where allowed to be told and their stories were allowed to exist in the same room. Meeting after meeting, the community heard stories of atrocities committed by the people working for the apartheid government and the African National Congress from the perspectives of the victims and of the victimizers. This is how Archbishop Tutu explains the reason for this third way of finding out the truth:

> [T]here were in fact different orders of truth which did not necessarily mutually exclude one another. There was what could be termed forensic factual truth—verifiable and documentable—and there was "social truth, the truth of experience that is established through interaction, discussion and debate." The personal truth—Judge Mahomed's "truth of wounded memories"—was a healing truth, and a court of law would have left many of those who came to testify, who were frequently uneducated and unsophisticated, bewildered and even more traumatized than before, whereas many bore witness to the fact that coming to talk to the commission had had a marked therapeutic effect on them.[12]

As the victims and the victimizers shared their stories, sometimes with inconsistent information and accounts, the bigger

---

[11]Desmond Tutu, *No Future Without Forgiveness* (New York: Doubleday, 2000), 30.
[12]Ibid., 26–27.

picture of what had really happened emerged. In trusting the ambiguity of their different experienced truths, the community, the people of the new South Africa, discovered that their real enemy was the system that persisted in valuing human beings based on their race and skin color. This kind of global truth-telling can help us restore and recognize our common humanity, moving toward healing and possible reconciliation and forgiveness. The real reality—the truth—is exposed, and now we can work together to transform the system.

The "healing truth" that Archbishop Tutu talks about is that divine truth that Jesus was testifying to. Archbishop Tutu names the purpose for telling the truth, which is to heal and not to continue the oppression. I have observed people telling what they considered to be the truth in order to hurt others. They tell the truth so that someone may be punished. They tell the truth so that they may justify their action in taking revenge or in gaining monetary remuneration. The motive for this kind of truth-telling is to win or to harm the other. In the end, there is still division between us and them, and no reconciliation or healing. Global truth-telling from both sides in these hearings was an essential part of the process of healing and reconciliation with accountability. It not only affirmed the victims' experiences by finally allowing their stories to be heard and believed, it also called for accountability from the victimizers in their confessions. It forced people from both sides to deal with one another as human beings and not as just oppressors and the oppressed, or as friends and enemies. The process of testifying to the divine truth invites us to tell our experienced truths in order to heal and transform our community.

The divine truth exposes the system of oppression. In testifying to the divine truth through global truth-telling, we begin to see something else at work that conditioned us to hate rather than love, to separate rather than to unite, to hurt rather than to heal. In testifying to the divine truth, we, the truth-tellers, begin to name the principalities and powers that seek to divide us. In exposing the oppressive systems—the principalities and powers—we make a differentiation between them and God. We begin to see that the world in which we find ourselves is not what God intended. We discover that God did not intend for humankind to be oppressed. God did not intend for humankind to be oppressors of one another. To know what is not of God is to begin to see who God really is. God's vision begins to emerge as we tell the truth.

God intends for all humankind to know that we are interconnected. We are members of one another. We are a community of people connected by the unconditional love of God. We are part of the body of Christ. In recognizing and revealing what God is not and gaining a clearer vision of God's intent, we ask the question, What does God invite us to do? We are then faced with a choice: to turn toward God—repentance—or to continue to follow the control of the principalities and powers. **The divine truth then becomes a divine judgment** that exposes and confronts oppressive systems by challenging the people in the systems to realign themselves with God's will. Jesus' death on the cross was the ultimate testament to the divine truth that exposes and judges the principalities and powers at work in oppressive systems.

In order to align our attitudes, words, and actions toward God's will, we have to let go of old ways of relating to others. We become like the Israelites, who had to let go of the way that the Egyptians had conditioned them to function as slaves and find the new way to live as a free people in the wilderness. We become like the early Jewish Christians, who, when they heard the experienced truth of the Gentile believers, had to let go of some of the Jewish customs and recognize them as not being essential to being a Christian, and find a new way to be in community with the Gentile believers. Through Jesus' death and resurrection, he has shown us that in dying, there is the promise of new life. Jesus gives us the courage to let go, to die to our old selves and find new life in Christ.

When we realign ourselves toward God's will, we restore the community of Christ as intended by God. We reconnect with one another across our differences, discovering the interconnectedness of humanity linked together by God's love and grace. This faithfulness, this unchangeable love of God—the truth—so perfectly shown to us by Jesus, requires us to trust God and therefore to trust one another to live in this new community in which we continue to testify to the truth. As we reaffirm our covenant with God, we covenant with one another to continue living in this new creation. We recommit ourselves to speaking and acting the divine truth by emulating God's nature and will—a pattern of truth-telling that invites dialogue that moves everyone toward reconciliation and new community, again and again.

> *[S]peaking the truth in love, we must grow up in every way into him who is the head, into Christ, from whom the whole body, joined and knit together by every ligament with which it is equipped, as each part is working properly, promote's the body's growth in building itself up in love…So then, putting away falsehood, let all of us speak the truth to our neighbors, for we are members of one another. (Eph. 4:15–16, 25)*

Ultimately, the divine truth restores the community of Christ.

In the summer of 2000, I was teaching an intensive five-day course on multicultural ministry. I enjoyed this format because I could take the time to get to know each student and explore each topic in depth without the usual running-out-of-time rush. Of the sixteen graduate-level students in the class, there were six African Americans, one Filipino, two international students from Sweden, and the rest were European Americans. On the third day, I observed a change of behavior in one of the African American students. His name was Mark. He was quiet and withdrawn all morning. From his body language, I could tell something was bothering him. I continued with my lesson plan, hoping that the course material would eventually "take care of it." I was in denial. During the morning break, I saw three other African Americans speaking with him. I thought to myself, "Let them take care of it. They know one another's background and culture much better than I do." I was avoiding my own guilt for not being an effective teacher, and certainly I was avoiding having to confront him.

Here was my interpreted truth as far as I could admit to myself. Based on my previous experiences, when an African American behaved in a withdrawn way, I had interpreted that behavior as disrespectful to me as a teacher. "What can a Chinese person know about the experience of racism against African Americans in the United States?" I imagined him thinking in his mind, "What can he possibly teach me?" In the early days when I started out doing diversity training and antiracism work, I had in fact encountered African Americans who expressed that view to me. It was also true that I did not understand very well the experiences of African Americans. It is still true now; I will be the first to admit that. But I still saw that withdrawal as disrespectful to my authority as a teacher. I could hear myself repeating a familiar complaint in my head, "Surely, there must be something they can learn from me! Don't dismiss me because of the way I look and not give me a chance to show what I know." My ego was getting in the way, as it does when I am insecure.

While all that was going on in my mind, at least I had the guts to admit that that was what I was feeling. When we returned from the mid-morning break, again I saw the same behavior from this student. "Okay," I said to myself, "I need to do something constructive now before this situation mutates into something unmanageable." I decided to start with a time of reflection and sharing from the students. I presented it as a time for them to share what they had learned from the class material and to ask questions. Just then, another African American student took this opportunity to throw me a lifeline. She said, "Something happened this morning in a small group discussion over there." She pointed at Mark's direction. "I want to know what happened, and I invite Mark to share, if you want to."

I knew this was the moment when the truth had to come out, not just from my own perspective but from Mark's and the rest of the class members'. I pulled out a chair and sat facing Mark inside the circle arrangement of the classroom. I was determined to just listen as empathically as possible without letting my own assumptions cloud my understanding of Mark. I was the teacher, and I was perceived to have more power. The divine truth begins with listening to the powerless, and therefore, in response to this challenge, I needed to listen. That was clear in mind: Practice what I preach. Even though I knew what I had to do, it still took every ounce of my energy to put my own assumptions aside so that I could truly listen to him.

"I don't feel I am being respected in this class," Mark finally disclosed his feelings. "I don't feel I fit in here. I'm the youngest person here and I'm from a different denomination from the rest of you. But I brought a dying congregation from sixty people to five hundred members, so I must know something."

There was silence. Everyone was anticipating what I was going to say. I decided to continue in my listening mode by asking an information-seeking question: "What was it that we did or that I did that caused you to feel disrespected?"

"You are the professor. What you said must be right." His statement caught me by surprise. "Back in the small group this morning when you joined us for the discussion, I shared some of my ideas, and you said something that was different from what I had in mind. It wasn't just this morning. Throughout the course so far, I have had very different ideas also. I figured that since you are the professor, you must be right and I must be wrong."

I responded, "So, when I shared my opinion this morning, you thought I was telling you that you were wrong, and you considered that as me not respecting you." I was in the feedback mode now to make sure I was hearing this correctly.

He nodded. I decided that this was my time to speak my experienced truth after listening to him. I said, "I am flattered that you respected my authority as a teacher that much. Here is how I might have a different perspective in terms of the teacher-student relationship. As a teacher, I have a lot of ideas, and some I am very passionate about. But as a teacher, I don't expect my students to agree with everything I say or believe. When I say something that is different from what you have in mind, that doesn't mean you are wrong. It just means that we have a difference of opinion. In this classroom, I expect disagreement, and it's not a matter of who is right or wrong, or who has the authority to be right and to tell others that they are wrong."

The cycle of listening continued as I now listened to Mark again. He then shared how he was brought up to believe that the teacher was always right and that as a student he had to respect that. I took the opportunity to connect our differences in perception of the teacher-student relationship with the "High and Low-Power Distance" cultural differences.[13] Having done that, I felt the need to tell the truth about what I felt. So I took the risk of telling the class and Mark that when I observed an African American behaving that way in a class I was teaching, it triggered all the old feelings of being told that I had nothing to teach

---

[13]See Law, *The Wolf Shall Dwell*, 13–28.

African Americans regarding the issue of racism. Mark then responded by saying, "That never even crossed my mind. You were the teacher; I have already learned a lot from you."

So the truth of our perspectives and feelings came out, not just from one side but from both. This more global truth informed us that we had misinterpreted each other's behaviors based on our own assumptions. When the truth was told, there was the possibility for reconciliation.

I asked Mark, "What can we do as a class to avoid this misunderstanding from happening again?"

He thought about it and then said, "Do like what we did. Talk about it honestly." I then made a covenant with the rest of the class to engage one another in this kind of honest, respectful truth-telling whenever we sensed that something was going on. That morning was the turning point of the class. The African American student who initiated this dialogue said, "I've never seen anything like this happen before. Usually the tension gets worse and worse, and we would have a big fight on our hands. I was wondering what you were going to do, and *wow*. Thank you." The divine truth restored our community.

On the last day of the class, I invited the class to participate in an exercise using photographs to share their images and ideas of God.[14] Out of the forty-eight photographs displayed, Mark and I happened to select the same picture: A man drawing a picture of a woman; in the photo, we see both the incomplete drawing and the model. When it was time to share our photos, I interpreted the photo this way, "I am like this man, the painter, and God is like this woman. I spend all my life trying to describe God to others like this man drawing a picture of this woman, but I am never one hundred percent there. It is always a struggle."

When Mark shared, he interpreted the photo this way, "I am like this model, and God is like this painter constantly trying to draw me and show me who I really am. I thank God every day for showing more of me each day I serve him." After everyone had shared in the class, Mark said, "Isn't it amazing that my interpretation of the photo is so different from Professor Law's."

---

[14]See Ibid., 115-20.

He looked at me smiling and concluded, "And that's okay." And we all said, "Amen."

At the crossing of Mark's perception of our teacher-student relationship and my interpretation of his behavior based on my previous experience, we refused to let the tension escalate destructively by separating us further apart. With the help of the community, we refused to let the principalities and powers of the world reinforce the destructive cycle of interracial relations. Instead, we chose to practice the "Cycle of Gospel Living,"[15] where the powerful—the teacher—lets go of control to listen, and the powerless is invited to speak. By affecting the power shift, we heard and understood the interpreted and experienced truths from both sides. We discovered in the truth-telling that neither one of us had the complete truth. In fact, we both misinterpreted the other's action based on our own experiences and assumptions. In the process, we exposed the principalities and powers that had conditioned us to think negatively of each other, to think the worst of each other, to repeat the old pattern reinforcing a myth that is not true about interracial relations. We can name the world around us together, and in naming it, we are able to commit ourselves to transform it. In the process, we forgive and reconcile to one another. We then covenant with one another, reforming a new community in which we can continue to testify to the truth.

Robert J. Schreiter, in his book *The Ministry of Reconciliation,* describes this restored community of truth well:

> Reconciliation means in the first instance, then, the cultivation of a relationship with God that becomes the medium through which reconciliation can happen. That relationship expresses itself in spiritual practices that create space for truth, for justice, for healing, and for new possibilities. Such practices lead to creating communities of memory, safe places to explore and untangle a painful past, and the cultivation of truth-telling to overcome the lies of injustice and wrongdoing. They lead also to creating communities of hope, where a new future might be imagined and celebrated.[16]

---

[15]Ibid., 63–70.

[16]Robert J. Schreiter, *The Ministry of Reconciliation* (New York: Orbis Books, 2002), 16.

Suggested Exercises

1. Take a biblical story and do a "power analysis."[17] Determine who in the story is the powerful and who is the powerless. Put yourself in the position of the powerless character first and reread the story. See and feel the story from that perspective. Write down your observations. Then put yourself in the position of the powerful character and read the passage again. See and feel the story from that perspective. Write down your observations. How does putting yourself in the position of the powerless first affect your interpretation of this story?

2. When dealing with an issue in your community, begin your exploration of the issue by listening to the powerless people in your community first. Then, listen to the perspective of the powerful in your community. How does listening to the powerless in your community first affect your understanding of the issue? After sufficient listening, write an imaginary dialogue between the two perspectives. Allow the dialogue to go on until there might be a resolution.

3. When studying a biblical story, ask the question, How does God see and act in the story? If Jesus is involved in the story, ask, How does Jesus see and act in this story? Follow up with the question, How can we emulate God's or Christ's action in our daily lives?

4. When facilitating a meeting in which you know there are differences of opinions, do a power analysis determining which group is perceived as the powerful one. Design an agenda in which the voice of the powerless in your community may be heard first, and then continue the dialogue by inviting the powerful to speak after they have listened. Make sure the dialogue continues for a few more cycles before inviting people to arrive at a conclusion as a community.

---

[17]For a fuller discussion on "power analysis" as a principle skill for leadership in a multicultural community, see Law, *The Wolf Shall Dwell,* 53–63.

Chapter 5

Angels at the Crossings

In 1978, I had just graduated from college and thought I had my future all planned. I already had gotten a job as a computer systems designer, which would start at the end of that summer. I would buy a car, find an apartment of my own, and go to work every day, living the free-spirited independent life of a young single American. In a few years, I might go back to graduate school to get a master's degree in engineering or business administration. When I told my friends at the Episcopal Church at Cornell about my plans, they were quite surprised. When I asked them why, one of them said, "I thought you were going to seminary."

Going to seminary was the last thing that crossed my mind. In fact, I did not even know what a seminary was. In any case, it got me thinking. At the recommendation of my priest, I decided to go on a five-day retreat that summer. I thought to myself that this would be a good way for me to prepare myself for my new life.

I arrived at the retreat center called Kirkridge—a beautiful setting on top of a mountain in Pennsylvania. It was going to be a nice relaxing week, I thought to myself. Then I entered the room where the group was meeting and discovered that the majority of the participants were over forty years old, and most of them were priests, pastors, and professional church workers from different denominations. What was I, a twenty-one-year-old, fresh out of college, doing here?!

However, the skillful leader of the retreat, a biblical scholar named Walter Wink, immediately made me feel at ease. I was respected for who I was and what I could offer in the Bible-study sharing time. Having grown up as the youngest child in a Chinese family, coupled with my immigrant experience, this acceptance was new to me. I knew that in that room I could say whatever was on my mind and I would not be judged as inexperienced, too young, too naïve, too Chinese, or stupid. By the third day, I felt such a high that there were springs in my feet as I skipped down the hill to breakfast, praising God all the way. In my newfound blessedness, I made a commitment that I would dedicate my life to the ministry of inclusion. From now on, I would accept everyone, love everyone, and welcome everyone. Like most twenty-one-year-olds, I was very idealistic.

That morning, Walter invited us to read the story of Jacob wrestling with a stranger (popularly known as an angel) until daybreak as he anticipated meeting his older brother Esau for the first time after he had stolen Esau's birthright years before (Gen. 32:22–32). As a way of getting more in touch with the story, he invited us to find a partner. In our pair, one of us would role-play the "angel" and the other would play Jacob. The one who played Jacob was to ask the angel for a blessing by saying, "Bless me!" and the one who played the angel would resist giving the blessing for as long as possible. The one who played Jacob would persist in this request and could use physical force if so desired.

I was sitting next to a man named Paul. He was in his forties and had had polio at birth. I had seen him navigate the slopes and hills around the retreat center on crutches. I realized that morning that I had not had a real conversation with this man. In retrospect, I might have been unconsciously avoiding any real contact with him because of my being uncomfortable with his disability. I felt awkward and a little ashamed as Walter gave the instructions for this intriguing exercise. I did not know what to do with the dissonance between my new commitment to be inclusive and my uneasiness with him as a disabled person.

After Walter finished the instructions, Paul looked up at me and said, "I guess I'm your partner." I smiled uneasily. "How on earth am I going to wrestle this guy?" I screamed silently.

"Why don't you be the angel first?" he said, as he stood up with the help of his crutches and faced me.

"Okay," I replied, without the slightest idea of what I was going to do. Now I was to bless this guy!

He looked at me in the eyes and threw his crutches away. With his arms outstretched in front, he started to fall toward me. "Bless me," he said.

My hands instinctively moved up to catch his hands as I felt his weight pushing me. I pushed back saying, "No."

"Bless me!" he said again with more force. I could not support his weight anymore, and we both fell on the carpeted floor. "NO!" I shouted as I fell.

I felt his calloused hands squeezing my fingers. His strong arms and shoulders worked together pushing me as he shouted, "Bless me!"

"NO!" I screamed without thinking what this exercise was about. I just needed to say "no." I could not accept him with his disability. I was uncomfortable with being around him. I could not bless him.

We tussled on the floor for quite some time with him yelling "Bless me" and my replying "No!" many times. And finally, in exhaustion, I stopped pushing and he did the same and our bodies, like magnets, came together—I held him tight and he, me. I didn't remember saying "I bless you" to him, but I believed he got my message in our embrace. I did remember feeling blessed by him however. In our wrestling with each other, our roles reversed. I, who was playing the role of the one to give the blessing, ended up being the one who needed his blessing the most. And I received his blessing of me with all my youthful awkwardness, my unconscious rejection of him, my willingness to just go with the flow of what others expected me to do—to follow the routines of life without question. In that blessing, I could see myself more clearly with my strengths and weaknesses, my yearning to be accepted as being valid, my willingness to fit in the roles that others had prescribed to me as a form of idolatry. In that moment of being blessed in spite of my imperfection, I got a glimpse of what God might have in store for me.

When we became aware of our surroundings again, the rest of the retreat participants were standing over us. They had finished their exercise a long time ago and were watching how we would resolve our wrestling on the floor. When we finally got up from the floor with their help, they applauded.

Sometimes in the crossing, when we think we are the one who is giving the blessing or offering the healing or being helpful, we might discover that we are instead the one who is in need of healing, blessing, and help. At the beginning of the retreat, I felt that I was a powerless person. But through the acceptance of the other retreat-goers and the leader, I experienced the joy of empowerment and blessings. In my blessed state, I felt free and empowered, with the feeling that "I can do anything I want." In my blessedness, I was shocked to discover that I was not living up to what I thought I should be—to be able to love and accept everyone. In my confusion at the crossing, I was not only wrestling physically with my disabled partner; I was wrestling with my own angel. It was as if there were two parts of myself—the part that knew I was good and blessed, and the other part that realized that I was fallen and in need of redemption. As the two parts of myself wrestled—the fallen-me struggled to gain acceptance, while the blessed-me resisted blessing the fallen-me—my internal struggles were physically expressed through my wrestling with Paul. In spite of my imperfection, I was still accepted and loved. In that way I received a blessing through him. I recognized that this struggle between the blessed-me and the fallen-me would be a lifelong struggle. Like Jacob, who went away limping because of a dislocated hip during the wrestling, I walked away from my wrestling with an acknowledged disability within myself—my inability to fully and faithfully follow God. This imperfection serves as a daily reminder that to be faithful to God, I need to wrestle with my own internal angel and the angels of our communities and institutions around me.

In the book of Revelation, in John's vision, Christ addressed the angels of the seven churches. As I read the letters in chapters 2 and 3, I began to notice a common pattern with at least five of the seven letters.

To the angel of the church in Ephesus:

> *I know your works, your toil and your patient endurance…*
> *But I have this against you, that you have abandoned the love*
> *you had at first. Remember then from what you have fallen;*
> *repent, and do the works you did at first. (2:2a, 4–5)*

To the angel of the church in Pergamum:

> *I know where you are living, where Satan's throne is. Yet you are holding fast to my name, and you did not deny your faith in me...But I have a few things against you: you have some there who hold to the teaching of Balaam...Repent then.* (2:13a, 14a, 16a)

To the angel of the church in Thyatira:

> *I know your works—your love, faith, service, and patient endurance. I know that your last works are greater than the first. But I have this against you...only hold fast to what you have until I come.* (2:19–20a, 25)

To the angel of the church in Sardis:

> *I know your works; you have a name of being alive, but you are dead. Wake up, and strengthen what remains and is on the point of death, for I have not found your works perfect in the sight of my God. Remember then what you received and heard; obey it, and repent.* (3:1b–3a)

To the angel of the church in Laodicea:

> *I know your works; you are neither cold nor hot. I wish that you were either cold or hot. So, because you are lukewarm, and neither cold nor hot, I am about to spit you out of my mouth. For you say, "I am rich, I have prospered, and I need nothing." You do not realize that you are wretched, pitiable, poor, blind, and naked. Therefore I counsel you to buy from me gold refined by fire so that you may be rich; and white robes to clothe you and to keep the shame of your nakedness from being seen; and salve to anoint your eyes so that you may see. I reprove and discipline those whom I love. Be earnest, therefore, and repent. Listen! I am standing at the door, knocking; if you hear my voice and open the door, I will come in to you and eat with you, and you with me.* (3:15–20)

The first thing to notice is that the letters were not addressed to the *people* of the churches. Instead, they were addressed to the *angels*. Walter Wink, in his book *The Powers That Be*, wrote extensively on this. He said:

[the] angel seemed to be the corporate personality of the church, its ethos or spirit or essence. Looking back over my experience of churches, I realized that each did indeed have a unique personality. Furthermore, that personality was real…But it didn't seem to be a distinct spiritual entity with an independent existence either. The angel of a church was apparently the spirituality of a particular church. You can sense the "angel" when you worship at a church. But you also encounter the angel in that church's committee meetings and even in its architecture. People self-select into a certain congregation because they feel that its angel is compatible with their values. Hence the spirit of a church can remain fairly constant over decades, even centuries, though all the original members have long since departed.[1]

He went on to say that the angel of an institution is also

the bearer of that institution's divine vocation… Corporations and governments are "creatures" whose sole purpose is to serve the general welfare. And when they refuse to do so, their spirituality become diseased. They become "demonic"…And if the demonic arises when an angel deviates from its calling, then social change does not depend on casting out the demon, but recalling its angel to its divine task.[2]

The pattern I saw as I read the letters is this: The angels of the churches were complimented for their good work that they had done in the past or at present, but then they were reprimanded for their unfaithfulness. Then there is a prescription for what they need to do. In other words, although the angels were good, they were also fallen and in need of repentance and a return to their divine vocation. Wink made the connection between the idea of the angel of an institution and the "principalities and powers," a term used in the Christian Scriptures, especially by Paul. He said, "What people in the world of the Bible experienced as and called

---

[1]Walter Wink, *The Powers That Be* (New York: Doubleday, 1998), 3–4.
[2]Ibid., 5–6.

'principalities and powers' was in fact the actual spirituality at the center of the political, economic, and cultural institutions of their day."[3] He went on to say, "Only by confronting the spirituality of an institution and its physical manifestations can the total structure be transformed. Any attempt to transform a social system without addressing both its spirituality and its outer forms is doomed to failure."[4] In order to transform an institution, we must address the angel, like the letters to the angels of the seven churches in the book of Revelation did.

> The Powers are good. The Powers are fallen. The Powers must be redeemed. These three statements must be held together, for each by itself is not only untrue but downright mischievous...They are good by virtue of their creation to serve the humanizing purposes of God. They are all fallen, without exception, because they put their own interests above the interests of the whole. And they can be redeemed, because what fell in time can be redeemed in time. We must view this schema as both temporal and simultaneous, in sequence and all at once...Conservatives stress the first, revolutionaries the second, reformers the third. The Christian is expected to hold together all three.[5]

The confusion that most of us have experienced at the crossings of differences challenges us to learn how to hold all three of these ideas about self and communities together in tension. In the prologue, I recorded my observation in the year 2002 regarding my nation, my church, and myself. I said that I was confused and paralyzed because I could not make up my mind about whether my country was good or fallen. In my effort in trying to make it clear, I got even more confused. Wink helped me live at the crossings with all of the conflicting passions therein. We are supposed to be confused. We are supposed to hold these confusing ideas, sometimes with opposing feelings and passions, in tension. We are supposed to address all of them sequentially and yet

---

[3]Ibid., 24.
[4]Ibid., 31.
[5]Ibid., 31–32.

all at the same time. As teachers, preachers, and leaders of the church communities, we are called to name our blessedness, our goodness as a community. We are also called to be courageous and to expose our fallenness. We are further called to make known the redemption through Christ and to call our communities to repent. Sometimes we do this sequentially over time; sometimes, all at once.

In a multicultural pluralistic environment, holding all three aspects of the angel of our community together, in tension, at the same time becomes even more significant. At the crossing of different cultures, different contexts, different values and myths, what one considers as blessedness, gifts, and strength in one context might actually be oppressive in another context. Living with and knowing what to do with our blessedness and the potential to be fallen at the crossing is the key to living faithfully in a multicultural pluralistic world.

Jack was a very powerful man, but he did not know it. He was a retired lawyer but still spoke with the clarity and power of one still practicing. Without being conscious of it, he dominated almost every conversation. Jack was also a faithful churchman. He had done every volunteer job there was during his fifty-years-plus involvement in his church. Jack was also a very smart man, quick to arrive at solutions and answers to analytical questions before anybody else. Most of the time, his perception was correct, but sometimes, when he was wrong, nobody would contradict him. He was part of a team of leaders from his church committed to attend a five-session antiracism multicultural ministry training. Among his team members was also his wife. During the discussion time early on in the program, when his wife was invited to speak, she would always defer to him, as if he spoke for both of them.

Jack's passion was social justice ministry. He served on the antiracism committee for his denomination. He offered his knowledge and skills as a lawyer effectively for this ministry. Jack was a European American who thought of himself as a liberal person who cared about the oppressed and the powerless in his community and in the world. But Jack was struggling with something that he could not put his finger on. He knew that with all his commitment and his talent, he was not making as great an impact as he would have liked in his work for social justice, especially in the area of racism.

As part of the training, each congregation's team was taught to use the Mutual Invitation technique as the principal process for sharing. Being forced to behave differently from his normal direct way, Jack began to see how he was being perceived by others in his group. After passing many times when invited to speak, his wife finally decided to speak out on the third session of the training. Jack for the first time realized that his wife actually had something to say. In fact, she disagreed with Jack on some issues. Jack was surprised. Why hadn't his wife ever said anything to him before? Why hadn't his team members ever verbalized their differences of opinion with him? He could certainly handle the disagreement. In fact, he expected people to argue with him when they disagreed. He considered that a respectful way to treat him. Something was happening to Jack—his angel was being exposed and challenged.

At the fourth training session, when I asked for a volunteer to lead the Bible study for his or her team, Jack offered himself for the job. I decided to observe his group. I admit that I had stereotyped Jack by that time, and I wanted to make sure that Jack did not dominate his group as a leader, especially during the Bible study. To my surprise, Jack followed the process closely. He did not deviate from it, nor did he interject whenever he wanted, as he used to do. When it came time for him to share—that is, when he was invited—he said, "I believe God is inviting me to shut up and let other people speak." There was a moment of grace when he said that. Jack had finally learned that by "being himself," he was dominating and sometimes oppressive to others.

Jack was a good person and saw himself as a liberator. Indeed, his conviction and commitment to work for justice showed that. His strength as an individualistic, outspoken, fast-thinking person had contributed greatly to that cause. However, in the course of the training program, he experienced a power shift, and for the first time, the truth was articulated by his friends and he heard it. He discovered that his greatest strength was also his weakness. His most treasured liberating skills were oppressive in an intercultural environment. His goodness was also his fallenness. And therefore, he needed to repent. He did that by choosing consciously to be silent.

Recognizing that I am good but also that I am fallen and need to repent is a continuous struggle at the crossings. We might have worked hard, might have accomplished a great deal, and might have seen and experienced the realm of God in our lives. We might think that we have arrived and can stay here, like Peter felt at the scene of the transfiguration, when he said, "It is so good here; let's build a tent for Jesus, a tent for Moses, and a tent for Elijah" (Mt. 17:4, author's translation). But Jesus calls us not to become lazy. The discernment does not stop when we have seen a glimpse of the realm of God. The struggle with the principalities and powers and angels does not stop. When we become too comfortable and relax and rely on past successes and blessedness and do not do the discernment needed at each crossing, we might allow our angels to stray from their divine vocation. Therefore, we must stay awake, for we do not know when the next opportunity for the realm of God to come upon us will be. We must stay alert and be ready to recognize when we might be fallen again and then take steps to repent and return to God.

A few months after speaking at the first interdenominational gathering of gay, lesbian, bisexual, and transgender (GLBT) Christians called WOW 2000 (WOW stands for Witnessing our Welcome), I was invited to write an article about racial issues in the GLBT community for *Open Hand* magazine. One of the reasons the magazine chose to focus on this theme was that during the event, a number of people of color felt they were excluded, even though the subject of the conference was on welcoming. As I struggled to articulate my thoughts on this topic, I found myself wrestling with a number of internal conflicts. Obviously there were complex issues involved, and therefore, to write about them in such a short form without trivializing the different perceptions is a difficult task. After struggling with this for a while, I decided to write my thoughts down in the form of a dialogue. This dialogue was between different parts of myself and is modeled after bits and pieces of conversations I heard at the WOW 2000 conference. The dialogue is between a gay or lesbian person of European background and a gay or lesbian person of color (indicated by dialogue in italics). To appreciate the full dynamics of this dialogue, read it with another person, each taking a part, like reading a play. Be sure to continue this dialogue by sharing your reflections with each other afterward.

WOW—A Dialogue

Place: An ecumenical conference for gay, lesbian, bisexual, and transgender Christians.

Time: Break time after a major keynote presentation.

Wow! Isn't it wonderful to see so many queer people in one place?

I suppose.

And we are all Christians! They can't really ignore us, can they?

I guess.

Hey, are you okay?

I don't want to talk about it.

Come on, you can talk about anything here. This is the most accepting and welcoming community I have ever been in.

How can you say that?

I thought it was a very good evening. In fact, I thought the whole conference so far has been so well put together. (Silence.) Okay, tell me what's wrong.

What's the use?

I want to know because I am on the planning committee.

Oh, God!

I'm supposed to find out how people are feeling about this conference and report back to the committee every night. (Silence.) How are we going to improve ourselves if you won't tell me what we did wrong?

Did you see what went on in there just now?

What? Which part?

When the speaker asked the people of color to stand up, to be recognized, a few people in the back yelled, "What color?"

I thought they were trying to be funny.

Apparently, quite a few people thought that it was funny too.

I guess it wasn't funny for you.

It was very offensive. And the speaker didn't do anything or say anything.

I didn't think they meant any harm. I guess they felt that since we are in this welcoming and accepting community, we don't need to make distinctions between color and race. You know, in Christ there is no Jew or Gentile, male or female.

But in this community, even though we are all GLBT, as we now say, there is still white and people of color. You can't get away from it.

We are gathered here as GLBT people—to support and encourage one another. Why focus on things that divide us?

But we're supposed to be a welcoming community, and yet I don't think the people of color here felt welcomed by what went on in there. Out of more than a thousand people in there, how many people of color did you see?

I don't know—about 50?

That's less than 5 percent. There must be more people of color who are GLBT.

I know. We really tried to recruit people of color to come. We sent out brochures to Christian communities of color. We even made sure we had people of color on the planning committee. I guess we can do better. Hey, you came.

I guess I am one of the naïve ones.

Naïve?

The rest of the people of color knew better.

What do you mean?

I thought that by coming here and being with all the gay and lesbian Christians, I would feel accepted. But judging from what I see, this so-called welcoming community is the same as any white community. It doesn't matter whether or not they are gay or straight.

I'm confused. I saw people of color as our speakers. Every time anybody up front spoke, they always included people of color in their remarks.

It's not what you say. It's a look here, a whisper there, and funny remarks like "What color?" that indicate to me that this community is just as racist as any.

Wait a minute. I wouldn't go as far as saying we are racist.

What would you call it?

We might be a little insensitive but...

If you don't believe me, talk to other people of color at this conference.

Don't you think you're a little bit too sensitive? I thought the whole racism issue was over with in this country.

I don't believe what I'm hearing.

Hey, at least the government has laws against discrimination based on race.

So, you think that by having these laws and policies, we have gotten over racism.

Yes...No...I mean, there is, of course, work to be done to make them enforce these laws. My point is that we, as GLBT people—we don't have the same civil rights in this country. People can say awful things and discriminate against gays and lesbians, not to mention bisexual and transgendered people, and there is no law to stop them. No one will dare to do that about race in public anymore. That's why we must stand together to work for justice for the GLBT community, just like we did in the civil rights movement in the sixties.

Yes, we must stand together and work together. But when we are standing together, we have to know and admit that there is racism even among us good-hearted welcoming folks.

Why are you buying into what the homophobic people want us to do?

And what is that?

Every time the gay and lesbian movement has tried to push a policy through in one of the mainline denominations, there have always been people who argue that if we accept gays and lesbians as *normal* people in the church, then we are rejecting the cultures of our ethnic Christian communities. They are saying that homosexuality is against the racial-ethnic minority cultures. So if we accept gays and lesbians, then we must be racist.

Maybe they are right.

They can't be right. To be gay does not mean I am a racist.

But the gay and lesbian movement basically was a white movement from the start.

Wait a minute.

Yes, the whole concept of coming out is a privileged white concept.

What?

All this talk about being courageous, being yourself, telling the truth and to hell with your family, your friends, or anybody who can't accept you—these are but ideas from very privileged people.

You've lost me.

In order to come out, you have to believe that you do have some rights as an individual to start with, am I right? And these rights are protected by society.

Right.

To believe that you have these basic rights is a privilege that is not shared by many people of color in this country.

You have as many rights as I do. The civil rights movement changed that.

We might have changed some laws, but people of color sure get checked at the airport more and still get stopped by police for wearing the wrong clothes in the wrong neighborhoods.

I guess there is something to that.

Because most of us don't have the basic rights to start with, we rely on our ethnic communities to support us. We don't have the luxury to come out, because in so doing, we risk losing what little security we have. That's why in many communities of color, we don't talk about who is gay or lesbian; we just know and we accept it. If we come out in public, that would give the racist system another excuse to take another shot at us.

All the more reason why we need to work together.

But as long as you want people to be out as the only way to be a good gay person, as long as there are TV cameras at this conference, as long as your mailing has your conference title on it, many people of color will not come.

With all due respect, wouldn't that be homophobic on the part of the communities of color?

No, that is your perspective. To us, the white gay and lesbian movement is not sensitive to our situations, our cultures, and our needs.

So, what do you suggest that we do? Affirm the homophobic people's position and let them divide us again and again?

No, work with communities of color on their terms. Support the GLBTs of color with the full appreciation of our contexts.

Okay, I can buy that. But this thing about making the distinction between whites and people of color—I still have a problem with that. While we are here, isn't there something we can do together?

I don't know.

You have to know that even though we are mostly white here, we do care about dismantling racism.

Yes, I don't question that. But again, it's not what you say, it's how you behave—which stems from your unconscious attitude—that counts.

So, what do we do?

I don't know. That's for you to figure out.

(Silence.) Liberation theology!

What?

Like the speaker said in the last session, as GLBT people, we are an oppressed people, but God is on our side. God will liberate us and empower us to bring justice to our people. Surely, we can work together on that!

That was another thing I had trouble with in the last session.

Oh, no. That too?

I'm not sure it's appropriate for a group of mostly white people in this context to talk about liberation theology.

We might be mostly white, but we are still oppressed as gay, lesbian, bisexual, and transgender people.

Okay, I agree that in the bigger scheme of things, the GLBT community should live and practice liberation theology. But in the context of this conference, when we are together as the GLBT community, who are the powerful and who are the powerless?

We are all powerless.

No, I mean, in these three days we are together, who are the majority, who are the ones with influence and power?

I guess the majority here is white.

Yes, so for the powerful majority to practice liberation theology is inappropriate.

But you can also say the same for gay men and lesbians who are the powerful majority in relation to the bisexuals and transgender people.

I would agree with you on that too.

So, it is not appropriate for gay men and lesbians to practice liberation theology too?

When they are working with bisexual and transgender people here.

If liberation theology is not the theology that most of us should practice here, what theology should we use?

(Silence.) What does Jesus say to the powerful and the rich in the Bible?

To sell what they have and give to the poor.

Take up the cross and follow Jesus.

How do we do that?

By letting go of control and power and listen.

Listen to GLBTs of color.

Yes.

Listen to the experiences of the bisexual and transgender folks.

Yes.

I have a proposal.

What?

I am the speaker for tomorrow's worship. I would like to invite you to speak instead.

What?

I want you to address the whole conference.

In front of a thousand people? Are you mad? What am I going to say?

Say what you just said to me in this conversation. I think everybody in the conference should hear that.

What will the organizers of this conference say?

They'll just be surprised, won't they?

Are you sure?

Yes. I am sure.

(Silence.) I have a proposal.

I really want you to do this.

Why don't we do it together?

No, as you said, they don't need to hear from me—a white person.

Yes they do. They need to know how we came to this decision— how you arrived at giving up your power so that someone like me can have a voice.

Wow. This is what liberation is about, isn't it?

Wow.

Power analysis is a concept I introduced in my first book, *The Wolf Shall Dwell with the Lamb.*[6] It basically means looking at a situation and determining who is perceived to have more power— power as defined by secular society, the ability to influence others

---

[6]Eric H. F. Law, *The Wolf Shall Dwell with the Lamb* (St. Louis: Chalice Press, 1993), 53–62.

and to manipulate the environment. This technique is used as a discernment tool to know how we are to speak and act depending on the outcome of the analysis. The gospel challenges the powerful to let go of power, to pick up the cross and follow Jesus. The gospel empowers the powerless to speak and act, because they are blessed, and God will liberate them. Living in a diverse community, power analysis becomes an essential tool. At every new situation, we must perform power analysis again to determine how we are to act. In our confusion at the crossing, power analysis points the way. It informs us of our blessedness when we determine that we are powerless in the situation. It informs us of our potential fallenness when we determine that we are powerful and might have the danger of abusing our power. Power analysis, coupled with the challenge of the gospel, prescribes what we are to do to steer ourselves and the angels in our midst back to the way of Christ.

> *For I do not do the good I want, but the evil I do not want is what I do. Now if I do what I do not want, it is no longer I that do it, but sin that dwells within me.*

> *So I find it to be a law that when I want to do what is good, evil lies close at hand. For I delight in the law of God in my inmost self, but I see in my members another law at war with the law of my mind, making me captive to the law of sin that dwells in my members. Wretched man that I am! Who will rescue me from this body of death? Thanks be to God through Jesus Christ our Lord!*

> *So then, with my mind I am a slave to the law of God, but with my flesh I am a slave to the law of sin. (Rom. 7:19–25)*

Aside from Paul's severance between the body and the mind, which scholars have studied and explored and expounded on for pages, I would like to focus on the internal conflict that Paul described. Is this not a similar struggle to what we have, living in a pluralistic world? When we think we are doing good, we might suddenly find ourselves doing damage to another group from another culture. I am not as ready to blame everything that is bad that I do on my body, as Paul did. But I am ready to acknowledge this struggle that I have faced, time and time again. How do I know I am doing the right thing? Sometimes, I hate myself for once again making a mistake and hurting another because I have unknowingly misused my gifts. How do I keep my angel and the angels of the communities to which I belong in check?

This is what it means to live at the crossings—a constant wrestling with angels. It is about knowing what the right thing to do is, based on past experiences, and at the same time being open to the possibility that you might be wrong this time. It is about having confidence about who you are and at the same time admitting that you might not know all of who you are. It is about knowing that you are a beloved child of God and yet having to live up to that title, knowing that you will not always succeed and that you will never be perfect at it. It is about knowing God and acknowledging that you do not know all of God at the same time. It is about being a saint and a sinner at the same time. It is about being sure and not-so-sure at the same time. It is about being powerful and powerless at the same time. It is about knowing you are good but fallen and in need of redemption—all at the same time. It is about being there in the realm of God already and yet still trying to get there. It is about living in the resurrection and then finding you must die again in order to gain new life, again and again and again. It is a cosmic struggle among angels as well as earthly struggles of power and resources. It is divine intervention as well as human cooperation. As we work hard each time to move toward the new creation of God through Christ, we must also recognize that there will always be traces of the ghosts of the past that threaten to pull us back and steer us away from God again.

As we struggle at the crossings, God also sends angels of a different order to minister to us. As the angel announced to Mary that she was to be the mother of the Christ child, we are called to be aware of the call to bear and give birth to Christ at the crossings. As the angel commanded Joseph not to be afraid to take the pregnant Mary as his wife, we are called to take courage to welcome and protect the powerless and outcasts at the crossings. As the angel ministered to Jesus after he was tempted by Satan, we are called to allow the angel of God to minister to us in our confusing and sometimes exhausting struggle at the crossings. As the angel announced to the women that Jesus had indeed risen, so we are called to proclaim the resurrection of Christ at the crossings by living out new possibilities, new creation, and new community.

Six months after the destruction of the World Trade Center, I finally found the courage to accept the invitation from my bishop to visit the site with a group of young people from Los Angeles. I dressed up as a priest with my black shirt and white collar. I was expected to minister to the young people—to be prepared to help them deal with the traumatic encounter. All the while, I was the one who was in need of pastoral care. I had had many opportunities to go down to the WTC site in my previous trips to New York to visit my mother and to work with the churches in the area, but I had avoided it time and again. Yet, there I was with a group of young people at St. Paul's Chapel, the Episcopal church closest to the WTC. The miracle at St. Paul's Chapel was that not a single window pane was broken, yet it was reported that there was three feet of debris piled up on top of the cemetery in the back. The church had been a place of rest and worship for the firemen and workers at the site. The walls of the church were covered with banners and letters of support and prayers sent by children from across the country and from around the world. It was a holy place where I felt out of place. While the young people were listening to an orientation presentation by one of the clergy working there, I wandered off to look at the letters and art around the sanctuary.

A fireman tapped me on my shoulder. I looked up and saw a broad smiling face. He extended his hand to me; I held it and immediately felt the calluses of his palm and fingers. "You're a priest, right?" He asked.

"Yes." I did not know how to react, so I did the standard thing. "I'm with that group of young people from Los Angeles."

"I thought you should have this." He reached into his pocket with his other hand and pulled out a piece of granite. He handed it to me. It was covered with dust. "This is a piece of the World Trade Center."

In my shock, all I could say was, "Thank you."

He then told me that he was a retired fireman. When he had heard about the attack, he went right down there to volunteer, and he had been there five days a week ever since. He told me that he had been digging every day, recovering the remains of those who had died. I remembered the calluses of his hands. He spoke as one who had seen the horror of the destruction, yet in a calm, you-do-what-you-have-to-do manner. As he spoke, I felt my fear and apprehension retreating. I sensed that I was coming back down to the ground of reality. At that moment, I realized that I had accepted the piece of the WTC that he had given me. I felt my palm and fingers being edged by the roughness of the granite from the tight clutch of my hand. I released my hand and looked at the stone. The dust from the stone stuck to the sweat of my palm. I realized that the dust was not just dust from the building. It was partly the ashes of the people who died. I cried.

"Thanks for giving this to me." I looked at him through my tears. "This really means a lot to me." I then introduced him to some of the young people from my group. They asked him questions and took pictures of his hands.

I held the piece of granite in my palm all through the eucharist later that day. I cried and prayed for the dead. I cried and gave thanks for the courage and dedication of the people doing the daunting recovery work. I cried and gave thanks to God for letting me know that even in the most devastating moment, at the heart of destruction, there is still redemption and hope. As I looked at the faces of the young people in my group, I thanked God for community in this time of sadness, anger, and uncertainty.

Later that day, after the worship service, I saw that same fireman sitting in a back pew with another fireman, talking quietly. I said to myself, "What an angel!"

At the crossing of my own fear and my own role as a pastor, I was tempted to hold on to my prescribed role and behavior as a priest, ignoring my own need and the needs of the others. I was tempted not to allow myself to feel the pain of those who had suffered and died. I was supposed to minister to others; but instead I was being ministered to by an angel—the retired fireman who gave me a piece of the WTC. The message I received was, "You do what you have to do with all the mixed emotion and confused passions. You do the best that you can based on what you know with all its fear and apprehension. That's okay with God. You might make mistakes; you might be broken down; you might even unknowingly hurt another; but in the end, God will send an angel to minister to you. You are blessed; you are fallen; and you are redeemable as a beloved child of God."

*I am convinced that neither death, nor life, nor angels, nor rulers,
nor things present, nor things to come, nor powers, nor height, nor
depth, nor anything else in all creation, will be able to separate us
from the love of God in Christ Jesus our Lord. (Rom. 8:38–39)*

Suggested Exercises

1. Select an issue that your community is addressing. In the way
    your community approaches this issue, how is your
    community good? How is your community fallen? What does
    God challenge your community to do?
2. Select an issue that your country is addressing. In the way your
    country is approaching this issue, how is it good? How is it
    fallen? What does God challenge your country to do?
3. Read a biblical text and ask these questions: How does this
    text affirm you and/or your community's ministry? How does
    this text challenge you and/or your community to be faithful?
    What does God invite you and/or your community to do
    through this text?
4. When working with members of a church community, invite
    each member to form small groups to discern the following:
    Name three strengths that the church possesses and three
    struggles that the church faces as it tries to stay faithful to God.
    After members have shared, invite them to write a prayer for
    the church community. End the gathering with each person
    sharing his or her prayer.
5. When working with a small group, invite each participant to
    name three gifts that he or she brings to ministry and three
    struggles that he or she faces trying to be a faithful Christian.
    After everyone has shared, invite the group to discuss the
    question, What can the community do to help its members
    with their struggles?
6. Construct a sermon or a lesson plan using these three themes:
    We are good and blessed.
    We are fallen.
    We are in need of redemption and a return to God.

Chapter 6

Preaching at the Crossings

As a fulfillment to my promise to my mentor Pierre Babin "to work with the poor," upon my return from France in 1981 I started working as a student intern at the Boston Chinese Ministry at St. Paul's Cathedral under the supervision of Fr. Benjamin Pao. The church community was made up mostly of refugees from Southeast Asia, with a few long-time upper-class Anglicans who came to the United States to retire. My first Christmas there, Fr. Pao invited me to preach. I saw this invitation as a great honor, and I worked very hard preparing the sermon. When I finished writing down my sermon the night before, I was pretty sure that it was going to be one of the best sermons that this congregation had ever heard. We let these egotistic things get in our heads when we are young. I started the sermon with the image of the baby Jesus, helpless and weak and vulnerable, and proceeded to give the entire story of Jesus' ministry. To me, the little baby in the manger evoked the whole of Jesus' message as the Messiah for the world. It was grand. It was a wonderful sermon, so I thought. It was even in Chinese.

The reception of the sermon was lukewarm at best. How could they not like my sermon on which I had worked so hard? Why couldn't they catch the vision that I saw? At my weekly supervision meeting, Ben said to me, "That was a very seminarian sermon." I was further insulted. Yes, I was a seminarian, but I learned great things at school and I was supposed to share them. I must have driven my supervisor crazy with my arrogance, even though it was a "stage" that I was going through, as they say. I had swung from being a very quiet, uncertain, lacking-self-confidence student to this extremely egocentric theological student. I guess Ben saw that, yet he let me be. One year later, Ben left his job to take on the challenge of starting a new church at the other end of the country. I, the seminarian intern, was now in charge of this congregation. "My God, why hast thou forsaken me?! What do I do now?" I screamed silently when he told me the news.

As far as I can remember, I continued to preach my "seminarian" sermons, and the people in the congregation were gracious enough to tolerate me. In retrospect, I realize that they really loved me and accepted me for who I was. In that acceptance, I too realized, and could eventually admit to myself, that the Sunday morning worship, with my scholarly preaching, was not working. Also, quite a few of the church members were not able to make Sunday morning services because they had to work. We needed something else to help us along. In one of the classes I was taking that year, we were studying the idea of base communities and home church. "Great," I said to myself, "Let's try that." So once a month, we would gather at the home of one of the church members on a Saturday morning. At these gatherings we would have food, lots of food—something that I discovered later was an essential element for any Chinese gathering. We would have our social time, and then we would sit together to study Holy Scripture.

Because these gatherings were not in church, the church members were in charge, and I became just one of the participants. Many of these homes were in low-income housing projects. Time and again, we found ourselves sitting on cardboard boxes and using plastic crates as chairs. However, the food that the members brought to share was always abundant. Somehow, at one of the early gatherings, I made a conscious decision not to talk too much, but to concentrate on listening to these wonderful people who I knew still loved me in spite of my incompetence as their spiritual leader. Instead of being in a teaching/leading/preaching/giving mode, I would listen to their concerns, their needs, their feelings, and their worldviews. The moment I decided to do that, I saw and experienced a world I had forgotten since I had started higher education in the United States. The sense of abundance that they shared, even though they had so little, was a treasure that I had lost and now had found. This abundance went beyond just food. They were teaching me, blessing me, humbling me.

At one of the gatherings, an older woman who seldom talked in Bible study classes or in church meetings shared her encounter with the Christian Church in China. With animated hands and sparkling eyes, she told story after story full of intrigue and adventure. Her conversion story captured everyone's attention in the room. I remember thinking to myself that her story said so much more than what I was attempting to do in my preaching on Sundays. There was the good news, right inside these people—people who knew they were beloved and who graciously shared this love abundantly with one another and with me. I remember thinking, while she was telling her story, "This must be what the kingdom of God is like." I finally understood why my mentor insisted that I come home and work with the poor.

The good news was not proclaimed by my word or my teaching but by my choosing to be silent and to listen. I, who was respected by the members of the church as their leader and therefore a powerful person, decided to take the powerless position, and in the process, the empowerment of the people occurred. Once we started the Saturday morning home gatherings, I began to preach sermons that were more relevant to the people in the congregation on Sundays. I found myself using stories and illustrations not only from what they shared but also from my own experiences. I knew I was connecting with them when they referred to a story or an illustration or a point I had shared in a sermon during casual conversations. For the first time, I knew that I was preaching with authority. This authority came not from myself or from my theological education, but from listening and receiving from the people whom I served.

As I reflect on what made my preaching different once I finally learned to listen, I discovered that I was more aware of the three cultural contexts that were at work in the community—the context of the people in the Boston Chinese Ministry, the context of the society in which they found themselves, and—more significantly—my own cultural context. Even though I was raised in Hong Kong and am ethnically Chinese and shared a great deal with the people of that community, I had very little understanding of their experiences as refugees of war. Furthermore, my education in the United States had, in effect, overshadowed my Chinese cultural experiences to the point that I was putting down everything Chinese in order to try to fit into the mainstream U.S. culture. Even though one of my objectives in working in the Chinese community again was to recover my Chinese heritage, I had to work hard to resist the instinct to reject that which was the Chinese way. I could not simply preach and teach assuming that I shared the same cultural context with the people in this ministry, even though we spoke the same dialect. Therefore, learning to listen to them was an essential part of my growth in becoming a better preacher and teacher.

When it came to the context of the mainstream United States culture, I had much more knowledge and experience, because I had been educated in the United States and had struggled to survive and gain acceptance in its cultural environment. As I listened to the people of the Boston Chinese Ministry, it brought back memories of my struggles in the early days of my immigrant experience. I realized that I did share this part of the experience with them. My preaching came alive when I utilized my knowledge and understanding of these three different contexts— the dominant culture of the United States, the experience of the Chinese refugees from war-torn Southeast Asia, and my confused state of being in between the Chinese and U.S. dominant cultures. My sermons weaved stories from all three contexts together. Sometimes these stories affirmed one another. Most of the time they were in conflict with one another, creating tension. The gospel came alive when it entered the picture to challenge, affirm, and resolve the conflict.

Before I started listening, I was using only what I had learned in seminary to create a sermon in isolation, without connecting that information with the multicontextual environment. My seminary education, especially the biblical studies classes, had taught me a great deal about how to interpret the Bible utilizing the various exegetical methods. But that alone was not enabling me to produce a good sermon. A good sermon must take into account not only biblical studies, exploring the contexts and meaning of the different texts in the Bible, it must also take into consideration the context of the community to which you are preaching, the context of society in which the community resides, and your own context. To know and understand each of these contexts begins with listening.

In a multiculturally diverse community, the task of listening becomes even more crucial because, within one community, there may be several cultural contexts that people bring with them to church. The values and assumptions embedded in these contexts might sometimes be in conflict with one another. To complicate things even more, these contexts may also be very different from the preacher's perspective and experiences. If the preacher does not spend time listening to and understanding these different contexts, he or she may be in danger of misusing his/her power and privilege at the pulpit. If the preacher spends time exploring these different contexts, he or she might notice that God through Christ may challenge one group but affirm another group in the same community. The preacher's message will find ways to connect with different people at different parts of the message. Obviously, this can get very complicated, and a preacher will never be able to connect with every context in every sermon. But the time the preacher spends listening to the different groups in the same community will become the foundational relationship between the preacher and the people. In a community in which the preacher really listens to the people, the preacher is not being judged for what he or she said or did not say. The preacher is accepted as a member of the community whose role is to put forth the truth and to highlight the good news for the community periodically as best he or she can do. Even though, at times, a specific group's perspective is not included in the sermon, the preacher is forgiven and loved still. I learned this concept of the preacher as a member of the community at the Boston Chinese Ministry. My sermons were not the greatest—I knew that, and they knew that too. But once they knew that I had worked hard to listen and to understand them, I simply did the best I could in my preaching. It was not about whether I was doing it right or not. It was about mutual feeding and empowerment. They had fed me with their abundant grace; I in turn preached that abundance back on Sundays.

A preacher has a lot of power and influence during the preaching moment in a church service. This power can be misused and abused if the preacher does not spend the rest of the week listening to, observing, and receiving from the people he or she serves. The powerful preacher must spend time to become powerless before he or she can preach with power and authority. If the preacher devotes his or her time to listening to the pain, suffering, struggles, challenges, joys, hopes, or fears of the people, when the moment of preaching comes, the preacher's words will speak the truth for the people in the community. Preaching is only one part of the dialogue between the preacher and the community. On Sunday, the preacher preaches and the people listen; during the rest of the week, the preacher listens, and the people preach; and the cycle starts over again.

Therefore, a primary discipline for us as preachers is to listen to the people in our church communities—not just those whom we like. Listen to the different cultural groups in your community—the different racial and ethnic groups, age groups, gender groups, economic groups, and so forth. More importantly, listen to the powerless ones in your church community first. Also, listen to those whom you do not like. Listen to your enemy. Obviously, you are not going to be able to listen to every group every week. But a discipline of listening to all the groups over time, both formally and informally, is essential for you to gain a deeper understanding of the different cultural contexts that exist in your community.

Put yourself in a listening mode whenever you are in different church gatherings during the week. Listen for the stories of your community, both present and past. Know their history, their myths, their values and beliefs, and the different ways they see the world. Know the recurring patterns of your community in the past. Know the angel of your church—how it is good, fallen, and in need of redemption. Are there different opinions and passions regarding different issues? Know the warring parties in your community. Be aware of what God-concepts drive the different groups. Learn the power relations among the different groups. If an issue comes up, whom would you listen to? Be sure to listen to the powerless group first. In a church community that has distinct cultural groups, you might want to develop a group of trusted leaders who have direct connections with the various groups. They can function as cultural translators, giving you information that you need and answering questions that you might have about particular groups in your community. One of the most effective ways to listen to the people in your community is to facilitate a weekly community Bible study group involving a diverse group of church members. The focus of the Bible study must be on listening to how each person connects with scripture and learning what concerns they have on their minds.

The second discipline is to listen to yourself. Be aware of your own feelings and reactions to different events in your own life, in your church community, and in society. Be able to stand outside of yourself and see yourself as others see you. Get behind the obvious and ask what caused you to feel or react the way you did. Be open to exploring events in your life that have impacted who you are. Be open to being surprised by what you might find out about yourself that you had not thought of before. Know your values, beliefs, and recurring patterns of behavior and thinking. Know the myths that drive you. Know your strength and weaknesses. Know your power and authority in relation to others. Know your angel—how it is good, fallen, and in need of redemption. Be aware of the God-concepts that drive you. Be open to other God-concepts that might bring out a different side of you.

You can do a lot of this self-listening and exploration alone. Some preachers keep a journal specifically for self-exploration. Some preachers have a disciplined quiet time daily to do this self-reflection. You can also do this self-reflection with the help of a spiritual friend or a spiritual director whose role is to enable you to reflect on and articulate this self-knowledge. As you listen to the different groups in your community, a side effect is that you will also learn to distinguish the differences between your context and theirs. This process of gaining self-knowledge should be a daily and weekly discipline if one is to be an effective preacher in a multicontextual community.

The third discipline is to listen to the society in which your church community resides. Read a local paper and a national paper. If you have access to one, read an international paper that might give you a different perspective on world issues. Watch a local television news program daily to find out what is going on in the local community. Watch a national television news program to find out what's happening around the world. Obviously, you are not going to be able to do all of that with the busy schedule of most preachers. But make it a discipline to do as much as you can, and if you notice that a particular issue was raised by what happened in the world and in the local community, do some research into the issue as part of your weekly discipline in preparation for preaching. Learn the power relations between different groups in your local community regarding this particular issue. Make sure you listen to the powerless groups in your society, because the discovery of the truth begins there. Get to know the beliefs and values widely held in your society. Know the history and myths of your local community and the nation. Know the recurring patterns of behavior and thinking of your nation as it has addressed different issues in the past. Know the myths that drive your community and nation. Know the angels of your local community, your state or province, your nation—how they are good, fallen, and in need of redemption. Know how your society views the people of your church community. Sometimes, the societal context may be similar to the context of the majority of the members of the church community. Sometimes, the societal context might be very different, or even at odds with the church community's context. This knowledge will inform you as to how and what you will preach.

The fourth discipline—the most important—is to listen to the scriptures. My own discipline is to read the lectionary texts at least one week before the Sunday when I will preach. Before doing any research on the texts, read and listen to them a few times. Listen for how these texts connect, affirm, or challenge you personally. What event or experience do these texts evoke in you? If you are drawn to one of the texts, write down some initial thoughts and do some research, such as exploring the literary, cultural, and historical contexts of the texts, and also do some word study. Hold them in your mind for the coming week as you listen to yourself, your church community, and your society. Watch for connections between the texts and the lives of the people in your church community. Pay attention to how the biblical texts affirm and/or challenge different groups in your church community. Watch for support and or challenges that the biblical texts issue for your society.

Eventually, you must sit down and record what you have heard in order to organize the data. I have prepared a set of worksheets for you to work through systematically each time you prepare a sermon (see Appendix). This process is graphically represented in the diagram below. The process involves walking though a labyrinth of the four areas of reflection. Each loop entails a five-step process of flushing out your learning in each context—observation, exploration, clarification, application, and communication. In the observation section, you write down those things that readily come to mind—the observable data and behaviors that you see,

Preparation Process for Preaching in a Multicontextual Community

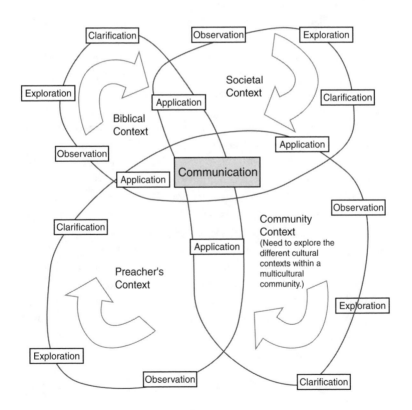

things that you hear and read, and so forth. The exploration section invites you to move deeper into discovering the values, beliefs, frameworks, and myths that might have caused the observable data. The clarification section helps you clarify what you have learned from the exploration. The application section asks you to consider how to apply what you have learned. Notice that when you are in the application stage of the reflection, you pass through the other three loops. You are asked how the more in-depth reflection in one loop impacts, informs, challenges, and affirms the other three contexts. The communication section invites you to decide what stories, themes, points, images, and arguments would be useful for your sermon. If you look at the diagram, you will find that the intersections of the four loops form a cross at the center. The material—stories, themes, points, images, arguments—that you uncovered at the crossing of the four loops will hopefully give you enough ideas to formulate a sermon.

Now that you have some themes, poetic images, arguments, and stories, you need to organize them into a sermon. I have included a number of typical patterns or outlines for a sermon. They are by no means all-inclusive. They are outlines that have worked for me in the past. Because of the differences in communication and learning styles[1] of the different groups in your community, a sermon should have a balance between poetic image and story-telling on the one hand, and clear argument, concept, point, and conclusion on the other. Each one of these sermon structures ends with the question, What is the good news? From my own experiences in putting together a sermon, asking this question at the end helps me refocus the work that I have put into the sermon so far. It brings everything back to God. What does the death and resurrection of Jesus Christ have to do with what you have been talking about in the sermon? How does the incarnation of Jesus empower us to follow God's will? How does God's unconditional love enable us to repent and return to God? What is the role of the Holy Spirit in helping us to live faithfully as a community?

---

[1] For a discussion on the impact of different communication styles on leadership and liturgy, see Eric H. F. Law, *The Bush Was Blazing but Not Consumed* (St. Louis: Chalice Press, 1996), 100–111.

Pattern 1: How does the gospel challenge and/or affirm us?
1. Begin with the biblical text. Explore the contexts of the text.
2. How does this passage challenge/affirm different individuals? What is a personal story that illustrates that?
3. How does this passage challenge/affirm different cultural groups in the community? What is a community story that illustrates that?
4. How does this passage challenge/affirm our society?
5. What is the good news?

(You can also reverse the order of challenges and affirmations, starting with society and moving toward individuals.)

Pattern 2: How does Jesus/God see it?
1. Take the biblical story involving Jesus and/or God interacting with people. Explore the cultural context of the people and their assumptions.
2. Distinguish between God's/Jesus' way of seeing the event and the people's assumptions and perceptions.
3. Correlate the people's assumptions in the biblical story with the assumptions of our community and/or society today. A story might be appropriate here.
4. How would God through Christ see our situation today differently from how we see it?
5. How can we realign our actions and words according to God's perception?
6. What is the good news?

Pattern 3: Correlate the experiences of the powerful and the powerless.
1. Begin with the Bible story. Do a power analysis with the different groups and characters in the text.
2. What does God require of the powerful in the story?
3. What does God require of the powerless in the story?
4. Correlate the experience of the powerful in your community and the powerful in the biblical story. What does God invite them to do? A story might be appropriate here.
5. Correlate the experience of the powerless in your community and the powerless in the biblical story. What

does God invite them to do? A story might be appropriate here.

6. How do the two groups work together in the community of Christ?
7. What is the good news?

Pattern 4: I am as confused as you are, but let's be faithful to the truth and listen to one another.

1. Describe an unresolved issue in your community.
2. Name and affirm the different opinions and perspectives about this issue. What should we do? Begin with the perspectives of the powerless group.
3. Connect with a bibilical text that describes the process of discerning the divine truth.
4. Tell a story that describes how a community or individual discerns the truth through this process.
5. Invite the members of the congregation to follow the pattern of discerning the truth.
6. Invite the members of the congregation to participate in a dialogue with others following this pattern.
7. What is the good news?

Pattern 5: Passionate but humble

1. Begin with the biblical story.
2. Tell a personal story about how you connect with the story. Pay attention to the sharing of your context. Be sure to let people know that this is just your own perspective based on your own unique context.
3. Tell another story about how another person or group connected with this story differently. Affirm the different connections as part of the process of discovering the truth.
4. Invite the members of the congregation to analyze their own contexts and how the story challenged and/or affirmed them.
5. What does the gospel invite them to do?
6. What is the good news?

Pattern 6: Prophetic

1. Start with telling the story and experience of a powerless group in your community. This requires the preacher to

listen to that community first and be able to represent its point of view in empowering ways.

2. Describe how the perspective of the powerless challenges the truth as presented by the powerful in the community.
3. Connect with the biblical text.
4. What does the gospel invite the community to do?
5. What is the good news?

The more experience I gained in preaching in a multicontextual environment, the more I moved toward what I call prescriptive preaching, as opposed to legalistic preaching. Legalistic preaching usually ends with the preacher telling the congregation what is right or wrong, or what is the truth. In a pluralistic environment, what is right for one group might be wrong for another. What is the truth for one group might not be the truth for another. Prescriptive preaching offers a way, a process by which the listeners can do some work themselves in order to discover what is right for them. The prescribed process refocuses the groups toward God, rather than toward the different groups' senses of right or wrong. The conclusion of a sermon might point to the truth as a process—what to do in order for diverse members of a community to reconnect with the gospel through Christ. In making that connection again, they decide together what they will do.

For example, during wartime, you might have members who are antiwar and members who support the war in the same church. What do you do? Is it possible for antiwar people and pro-war people to coexist in one body? If you preach according to your own conviction, you might alienate one group or the other. If you do not preach your own conviction, then you're not true to yourself. In your preaching, demonstrate your own struggle with the scriptures and arrive at your own conclusion. But be sure to let the congregation know that this is just your own perspective and your own conclusion. The sermon should continue by issuing an invitation for the people to bring their own contexts to bear and to arrive at their own conclusions as to what they will do. The final invitation, if you know there will be differences in opinions, is for them to engage one another in dialogue, because it is through dialogue that we may discover the truth together.

In other words, preach the truth—which is the process that models the pattern of Christ's approach to issues. And let the divine truth make the judgment, not you. Let the gospel be the prophetic utterance, not you. For I truly believe that if we redirect the energy of a diverse community toward the center, the gospel of Jesus Christ who is the way and the truth, conviction and reconversion will happen. Your job as the preacher is to showcase the gospel and to provide the invitation and the process for them to enter into discovering the divine truth. Therefore, this way of preaching must be accompanied with educational opportunities for people to continue their learning and discernment of the truth, which is the subject of the next chapter, "Teaching at the Crossings."

Chapter 7

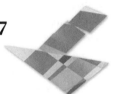

Teaching at the Crossings

For six years you shall sow your land and gather in its yield; but the seventh year you shall let it rest and lie fallow, so that the poor of your people may eat; and what they leave the wild animals may eat. You shall do the same with your vineyard, and with your olive orchard. (Ex. 23:10–11)

You shall count off seven weeks of years, seven times seven years, so that the period of seven weeks of years gives forty-nine years…[Y]ou shall have the trumpet sounded throughout all your land. And you shall hallow the fiftieth year and you shall proclaim liberty throughout the land to all its inhabitants. It shall be a jubilee for you: you shall return, every one of you, to your property and every one of you to your family. That fiftieth year shall be a jubilee for you: you shall not sow, or reap the aftergrowth, or harvest the unpruned vines. For it is a jubilee; it shall be holy to you: you shall eat only what the field itself produces. (Lev. 25:8, 9b–12)

A seminary professor at a conference for clergy was giving an address on the concept of Jubilee and Sabbatical years from the Hebrew Scriptures. He spoke as if the prescribed actions and practices were for everyone to follow. The speaking style of this seminary professor reminded me of my seminary days when I used to question anything that came my way, especially when there was a claim of universality. At the end of his presentation, I raised my hand and asked, "To whom is this stuff about forgiving debts and releasing the slaves and captives addressed?" Of course, this was a rhetorical question for which I already knew the answer.

The question seemed to catch him by surprise initially. I was hoping that he would say "for everyone," so that it would give me the reason to come back with my answer. But the scholar caught on to where I was going and gave me the answer I had in mind. He said, "I guess the prescription of behavior for Jubilee and Sabbatical years was for those who had power and owned land."

Having been disarmed, I then followed up with this question: "While the rich and powerful people are still trying to get the idea of Jubilee—which, by the way, was never fully realized—what should the poor and the have-nots do?" In spite of my mischievous behavior, I believed my question was still a valid one. The professor did not have time to fully address that. But I will return to this question later in this chapter.

During the social time after his presentation, I apologized to the speaker for my "disrespectful" behavior. But the idea that the prescribed commands for the Sabbatical and Jubilee years were written for those who have power lingered with me and caused me to further explore it. After the Israelites entered Canaan, they settled into a way of life that included those who owned land and livestock and hired servants, and slaves who, for some reason, did not have land of their own and had to rely on serving and working for a living. In some way, the weekly Sabbath, the Sabbatical year, and the Jubilee year as commanded by God for Israel to keep were God's way of anticipating the eventual power differentiation that would exist in the settled community. The Sabbath was a commandment that ensured that in the newly formed community, those who had no power and resources might be protected from being abused and would be guaranteed a time for rest and relief from work. This required the powerful and rich to follow Sabbath as a discipline and give their workers rest every seven days.

In the Sabbatical year discipline, the powerful were to let go of control of their land and resources every seven years to allow the poor and the animals in nature to share the abundance of the land. Jubilee took this discipline even further by providing a vision that invites the whole community to start over again without the constrained relationships based on roles imposed by the current system. Jubilee invited the powerful and rich to forgive the debts of those who owed them, to free the slaves that served them, to open up the boundaries of their land and allow others to enter and share that abundance. Even though Jubilee was never fully realized, it remained a continuous challenge, especially to the rich and powerful in Jewish society. The first thing that Jesus did at the beginning of his ministry was to proclaim Jubilee. Through his ministry to realize Jubilee, Jesus not only affirmed the blessedness of the poor and powerless, he also challenged the powerful and rich again and again to give up what they had, to take up the cross, and to follow him. At the most basic form, the weekly Sabbath, the Sabbatical year, and the Jubilee were a discipline for the powerful to open up their boundaries and encounter others anew, without the prescribed roles and power relationships imposed by society but rather as children of God. I like to think of Sabbath and Jubilee as a principal part of what I call "a pedagogy of the powerful."

Over the years, I have consulted with a variety of organizations and communities that wanted to learn to embrace diversity and become more inclusive. As a discipline, I always evaluated each one of these consulting relationships at the end of the process so that I could learn from my successes and failures. I would consider my work with an organization to be a failure when I did not see any constructive change toward becoming a more inclusive community at the end of the consulting relationship. As I examined these "failures" more closely, I concluded that one of the reasons why very little change had occurred was that these organizations did not commit themselves to practicing Sabbath.

I see the workshops on diversity and building inclusive community as an invitation to Sabbath. The invitation is for people at different levels of the organization to stop doing what they do every day and take a rest. In this resting time, they are invited to open up their boundaries and step out of their prescribed roles so that they can encounter and relate to others as fellow human beings—children of God. Together, with their learning from truly encountering one another, they can find new and more inclusive ways to be in community. In order for this to happen, the power holders of an organization must be willing to allow the members of the organization the time and space to do this. That is, the leaders of the organization must give the people Sabbath. When the power holders of the organization refuse to do that, the chance for real, constructive change diminishes. For example, after an initial workshop I had given to one such community, I invited members to sign up for additional workshops, so that the community could have more time to further address their diversity concerns. I got enough responses to agree to come back for a full day of workshops. When I returned one month later to give the workshops, only two or three persons showed up for each of the workshops. When I encountered some of the managers in the hallway, one after another gave me excuses as to why he or she was not able to come to the workshops. The most popular excuse was "I'm too busy. I have no time." Since the upper management level did not honor the time they had committed to the consulting process, the rest of the employees did not bother to come either. When an organization, particularly those who have power, does not honor the need for Sabbath, there will be no opportunity to learn and encounter others, and very little will change.

The first step to the pedagogy of the powerful is to teach them to honor Sabbath by committing the necessary time, not just for themselves but also for the powerless. The second step is to teach them what to do during this sabbatical time.

> Observe the sabbath day and keep it holy, as the LORD your God commanded you. Six days you shall labor and do all your work. But the seventh day is a sabbath to the LORD your God; you shall not do any work—you, or your son or your daughter, or your male or female slave, or your ox or your donkey, or any of your livestock, or the resident alien in your towns, so that your male and female slave may rest as well as you. Remember that you were a slave in the land of Egypt, and the LORD your God brought you out from there with a mighty hand and an outstretched arm; therefore the LORD your God commanded you to keep the sabbath day. (Deut. 5:12–15)

Just what are we supposed to do on the sabbath day? Once we stop working and walking in our prescribed routines, how should we spend our time? Notice in the Deuteronomy text, male and female slaves, sons and daughters, livestock, and resident aliens are named specifically as ones who may rest on the sabbath day. When people of different status and power roles are all asked to stop working, I believe God's intention is for us to start encountering one another as just people and not as our roles in our families, at work, and in society. Sabbath is a time for us to stop doing what we usually do and encounter others who are different—from another land, class, age. Sabbath is God's invitation to enter the crossings to truly encounter others. In that sense, Sabbath is the crossing.

From the Deuteronomy text, we are also told to "Remember that you were a slave in the land of Egypt, and the LORD your God brought you out from there with a mighty hand and an outstretched arm; therefore the LORD your God commanded you to keep the sabbath day." The purpose of the Sabbath is to remember what God has done for us. Sabbath is a time to reconnect with God, to remember, and to learn to be faithful to God again. God knows that we, humankind, will forget and will rebel, sin, and distance ourselves from God again. Sabbath is a disciplined time in which we encounter who we really are and what we have done, and we discern whether we are following God or not. This process of turning back to God—repentance—is intimately related to the command to stop working so that we can step out of our boundaries to encounter others—especially those from different classes, those of a different age, and those whom we have considered "foreigners." At the crossings of our differences, we learn the truth by listening to those who are powerless. In discovering the truth, we are confronted with how we have not followed God's commandment to love our neighbors. We then recommit ourselves to steering our lives back toward following God again.

> *Just then there came a man named Jairus, a leader of the synagogue. He fell at Jesus' feet and begged him to come to his house, for he had an only daughter, about twelve years old, who was dying.*
>
> *As he went, the crowds pressed in on him. Now there was a woman who had been suffering from hemorrhages for twelve years; and though she had spent all she had on physicians, no one could cure her. She came up behind him and touched the fringe of his clothes, and immediately her hemorrhage stopped. Then Jesus asked, "Who touched me?" When all denied it, Peter said, "Master, the crowds surround you and press in on you." But*

Jesus said, "Some one touched me; for I noticed that power had gone out from me." When the woman saw that she could not remain hidden, she came trembling; and falling down before him, she declared in the presence of all the people why she had touched him, and how she had been immediately healed. He said to her, "Daughter, your faith has made you well; go in peace."

While he was still speaking, someone came from the leader's house to say, "Your daughter is dead; do not trouble the teacher any longer." When Jesus heard this, he replied, "Do not fear. Only believe, and she will be saved." When he came to the house, he did not allow anyone to enter with him, except Peter, John, and James, and the child's father and mother. They were all weeping and wailing for her; but he said, "Do not weep; for she is not dead but sleeping." And they laughed at him, knowing that she was dead. But he took her by the hand and called out, "Child, get up!" Her spirit returned, and she got up at once. Then he directed them to give her something to eat. Her parents were astounded; but he ordered them to tell no one what had happened. (Lk. 8:41–56)

Jairus was a ruler of the synagogue, a powerful man. His only daughter, twelve years old, was dying. The nameless woman, who had had a flow of blood for twelve years, was a powerless person who was considered unclean and therefore an outcast. The offspring of the powerful was dying and in need of the healing of Jesus. But on the way, it was the powerless that needed to be healed first before the powerful could be revived. In the drama of the story, after the woman had touched Jesus' garment, he felt that his power had gone forth from him. One could imagine and hear Jairus and his friends thinking, "Oh no, Jesus just used up his healing power! He will not have any left for Jairus' daughter!" Some might even have thought, "Why is a lowly, unclean woman stealing what rightfully belongs to the ruler of the synagogue?"

The drama continued with the report that Jairus' daughter had died while Jesus was commending the faith of the unnamed woman. This confirmed the fear of the rich and powerful: that there is only so much limited wealth and resources, and once it is used up, there will be no more. With that fear, the rich and powerful in most societies have used their power to maintain their wealth and resources; and more importantly, they continue to accumulate more, because one never knows when it might run out or be taken away. In the process of trying so hard to keep what we have and to gain more, there is a spiritual dying—the inability to see the abundance of God's love, grace, and creation. In the story of Jairus' daughter, even though the powerful finally acknowledged the need for healing, and saw the answer to this healing in Jesus, they still operated out of fear and scarcity.

But wait. Jesus' healing power did not dissipate, even though the unnamed woman had been healed. He went on to heal Jairus' daughter anyway, even after they laughed at him for saying that she was not dead. Jesus healed Jairus' daughter not because they had faith, like that unnamed woman. He healed her to prove a point—that God's healing power is not limited like the power and wealth that the powerful have tried to accumulate and keep. The story of Jairus' daughter shows us two things about the pedagogy of the powerful:

1. The pedagogy of the powerful must be preceded by the encountering and the healing of the poor, the rejected, the outcast, and the powerless. Jesus took a little Sabbath, stopped what he was doing for the powerful, and affirmed the faith and the healing of this poor outcast woman. It is like a detour, a Sabbath that must happen before the powerful can be made whole.

2. The pedagogy of the powerful must include teaching them that God's healing power is not a limited resource like their own money, power, and resources. Instead, God's abundant love, forgiveness, grace, and healing is always enough for everyone who believes.

So often, when teaching and preaching the gospel to the powerful, we only cite the passages in the Bible when Jesus challenges the rich and powerful to give up what they have and give to the poor. The challenge to let go is indeed a primary message for the powerful. However, that is not the complete message. If we just issue the challenge and leave them there, they might lose hope and become paralyzed. If we still do not follow up and address their sense of hopelessness, they might eventually give up trying to respond and might even act in ways that are counterproductive. For example, for many years I participated in antiracism training in which we forced the historically dominant cultural group to face the history of oppression and to recognize their privileges. We pointed our fingers at them and called them oppressors. We asked them to let go of their power. Very often, we left them there in a state of powerlessness where they might be afraid that because they had given up their power and let go of control, there would be nothing left for them. When that happened consistently to them, some of them eventually gave up coming to any of these kind of events. Worse, some of them now actively work against having such trainings and workshops again.

The challenge to let go of their power must be accompanied by the message of grace. The message is that God will still love them, even if they don't have any power. Jesus said that the first shall be last. But he did not say that the last do not get to be loved and welcomed. Jesus said that when you are invited to a banquet, don't sit at the seat of the honored guest. But Jesus didn't say that you don't get to eat and enjoy the party. In order for the rich and powerful to discover who they are, stripped of their power and possessions, they have to know the love of God abundantly. With the assurance of the love of God, the powerful can have the courage to let go of their power. They would follow the disciplines of Sabbath and Jubilee and open their boundaries to share their resources with the poor and the outcast. They then might allow themselves to be open to learning, seeing the world not just from their own limited points of view, but from the perspectives of the powerless and the oppressed. They might learn to use their power to make Sabbath happen for those who have worked for them. At Sabbath, instead of being paralyzed, they will have hope as they learn to discern the truth again and again.

Rev. Johnson, as he insisted on being called, was a gifted and powerful preacher in his fifties. His identity as a preacher had somehow overtaken the way he communicated, not just in the pulpit but in his everyday conversations. He had decided to spend a week on retreat in a very diverse setting with men and women of different ages and races and ethnicities. I was the retreat leader. For five days, the daily discipline included studying scripture for part of the morning, with the rest of the morning activities addressing racism and diversity. Everyone had the afternoon off, with no planned program. This would be the time for silent reflection, hikes in the beautiful wooded setting, and conversations with others. At the end of the day, the participants rejoined their morning Bible study groups to reflect on what they had learned during the day. The process we used for sharing in both the Bible study time and the evening reflection was the Mutual Invitation process, in which each person is invited to speak without being interrupted. They also affirmed daily a set of communication guidelines that reminded them to respect what they heard and to keep confidentiality.

On the first morning, when Rev. Johnson was invited to share his thoughts on the Bible passage, he proceeded to give a sermon. The facilitator had to stop him and gently remind him that there were other people who needed to be allowed to speak, and each person had to be aware of how much time he or she was using in order to respect other people's time. He was willing to comply.

By the third day, Rev. Johnson seemed to have gotten used to the Mutual Invitation process. He seemed to be more relaxed and not as anxious to jump into the conversation. He became more and more quiet each day. In fact, he was listening quite attentively to the women, young people, and persons of color in his circle. Not only that, his verbal sharing began to shift from a traditional preaching tone to a more personal sharing style. That is, instead of saying "we should" or "let us," he was beginning his sharing with "I feel."

At the end of the conference, I gathered the facilitators to debrief them and to collect feedback. The facilitator for Rev. Johnson's group said, "I have never seen a grown man cry—a preacher at that. During the last session, he said that for the first time, he had realized what he had to do in order to undo racism. For the first time, he was not stuck, but had hope."

Through the discipline of the week, Rev. Johnson, a powerful preacher, had moved from the active mode of speaking to that of listening. He was experiencing Sabbath, in which he finally stopped playing his prescribed role. He was willing to open up his mind, his boundary, and to allow others in. As a result, he was able to hear the others' experiences and see a more complete reality that included the vision and voice of the powerless. In confronting this reality while experiencing the graciousness of the environment, the Word was made known to him, and he experienced conversion.

He was no longer paralyzed by guilt. He could look toward the resurrection with hope.

Here is a summary of the pedagogy for the powerful based on my own experiences of working with those who have power and influence in communities and organizations:

1. Invite them to honor Sabbath in the form of committing the time necessary for them to step outside of their prescribed power roles and to encounter others. This commitment is crucial for the pedagogy of the powerful. Not only do they need to commit the time for themselves, they must also use their power and influence to make Sabbath time for others in the community. Sometimes this must be done formally, such as asking them to sign a covenant committing themselves to participate in a series of programs. Be very clear about the time commitment required. Also, if they think the time asked for is too much, you then need to negotiate for an agreeable amount of time that they can definitely commit to. It is better to begin with a short time than to force them to agree to an unrealistic commitment, which would result in their not participating.

2. State clearly to them the parameters of the program in both behavior and content at the beginning of the program. For behavior, present a set of respectful communication guidelines and invite them to agree to uphold them. For content, do a process by which they are asked to name their fears if they were to engage themselves in the discussion of the topic of the program. Ask them what would need to be said and done in order to bring them to a safer space in order to address the topic at hand. In other words, create a grace margin.[1]

3. As part of the process to create the grace margin, begin every gathering with Bible study. Invite them to practice

---

[1] I described the concept of the "grace margin" in Eric H. F. Law, *Inclusion* (St. Louis: Chalice Press, 2000), 39–48. I provided a process for a small group of church leaders to arrive at the first step of the process called "drawing the parameter" in Law, *Sacred Acts, Holy Change* (St. Louis: Chalice Press, 2002), 104–10.

listening to one another's reflections and connection with the scriptures. The most effective technique is the process of Mutual Invitation. Each time, ask them to reflect on what God is inviting them to do, to be, or to change through the passage. Emphasize the importance of listening first for the powerful theologically. I usually make sure that one of the passages being studied is the Pentecost passage, in which the powerful in the story were challenged by the Holy Spirit to listen.[2]

4. Invite them to participate in processes and activities to explore their own internal cultures. For the historically powerful group in any community, their internal culture is often the same as the environment's culture, because they were the ones who shaped it. They might think of their assumptions, beliefs, or values as the norm and take for granted the privileges that they have. By being engaged in activities that expose their individual internal cultures—their unconscious beliefs, values, patterns, and myths—they can acknowledge their own personal cultures and learn not to assume that these cultures are universal. In terms of a particular issue, invite them to describe their individual reactions and perspectives, and then invite them to explore further into their internal cultures by asking these questions: What caused you to feel this way? What assumptions, beliefs, and values do you have regarding this issue? The more they can acknowledge their own values and beliefs, the less likely they are to be defensive and will therefore be open to listen to a different perspective.

5. All the above steps are but preparation for them to enter the crossing to encounter the others who are different—especially the powerless. This needs to be coordinated with the facilitators working with the powerless. During the encounter, the first thing to do is to have a Bible study together, again making sure there is mutual listening.

---

[2]See Eric H. F. Law, *The Wolf Shall Dwell with the Lamb* (St. Louis: Chalice Press, 1993), 45–52, 71–78.

When addressing the topic of discussion, invite the powerful to listen first, because discerning the truth begins with the powerless. This may be as simple as inviting the powerless group to go first in the process of sharing.

6. After they have listened, invite the powerful to speak, based on what they have heard. This is an important step, because a fear that the powerful have is that once they have given up their control and power, they will not get it back. This continuation of the communication cycle is a way of indicating to them that they are not shut out of the dialogue forever. There will be time for them to share their thoughts only after they have listened first.

7. As the fuller, more complete description of the issue—the real reality—emerges, the dialogue needs to shift its focus toward God. We ask, Is this reality what God intended for this community? How would God through Christ see this situation? What does God through the gospel of Christ call us to do? The confrontation of the powerful comes at two places. First, when they are able to listen to the side of the story of the powerless, they might discover that the way they exercise power may have a negative effect on the powerless. Confronted with this more complete realty, they may decide to change the way they use their power in order to correct the situation. Second, when the powerful are confronted with how the exposed reality is not in congruence with God's vision, they are then called to work with the powerless to steer the community to return to God.

Let me return to the question I posed for the conference speaker at the beginning of this chapter: "While the rich and powerful people are still trying to get the idea of Jubilee, what should the poor and the have-nots do?" What does the pedagogy for the powerless look like?

The year 2002 was the year when Juan Diego became the first Native American to be canonized as a saint in the Roman Catholic Church. It was almost five hundred years after the event in which he encountered the divine revelation through the Lady of Guadalupe at Tepeyac before the church was willing to recognize the significance of Juan Diego's role in this important event. One of the reasons it took so long was that there were disputes as to whether Juan Diego actually existed; perhaps he was just a legend. But one cannot ignore the impact of Our Lady of Guadalupe in the Americas. The story of Juan Diego is worth retelling here for the benefit of those readers who do not know the story. The summary below (with actual text in quotes) is based on Virgil Elizondo's extensive study of the Guadalupe event in his book *Guadalupe—Mother of the New Creation*.[3] As you read the story, be aware of the power positions of the characters and how the divine presence interacted with them. Whether you believe this actually happened or not, the story itself tells the divine truth that I have described in this book.

In 1531, ten years after the conquest of Mexico by Spain, "Everywhere the inhabitants of the lake and the mountain had surrendered." The church had worked diligently to convert the Indians to Christianity. But under this political backdrop, any transference of the faith was tinted by the emancipation of the native way of life. Nevertheless, Juan Diego had been faithful in following the teaching of the church. He was described as a poor and dignified person. He lived in Cuautitlán, and on a Saturday night, he was on his way to Mexico City to receive his instructions from the priest. At the side of the small hill named Tepeyac, "he heard singing on the summit of the hill: as if different precious birds were singing and their songs would alternate as if the hill was answering them." When the song ceased, he heard someone calling him. He followed the voice and saw a lady whose clothing "appeared like the sun, and it gave forth rays." She asked him, "Where are you going?" He explained that he was going to Mexico City to receive instructions from the priest. There she gave her first instruction:

> I very much want and ardently desire that my hermitage
> be erected in this place. In it I will show and give to all
> people all my love, my compassion, my help, and my

[3]For the full translation with commentary on the Nican Mopohua, which tells the story of the Guadalupe event in verse, see Virgil Elizondo, *Guadalupe, Mother of the New Creation* (New York: Orbis Books, 1997), 1–22.

protection, because I am your merciful mother and the mother of all the nations that live on this earth who would love me, who would speak with me, who would search for me, and who would place their confidence in me. There I will hear their laments and remedy and cure all their miseries, misfortunes, and sorrows. And for this merciful wish of mine to be realized, go there to the palace of the bishop of Mexico, and you will tell him in what way I have sent you as a messenger, so that you may make known to him how I very much desire that he build me a home right here, that he may erect my temple on the plain.

He readily accepted the mission and went to the palace to seek the ear of the bishop—Don Fray Juan de Zumárraga. With some difficulty, he finally got to see and tell the bishop what he had admired, seen, and heard. But the bishop answered him, "My son, you will have to come another time; I will calmly listen to you at another time. I still have to see, to examine carefully from the very beginning, the reason you have come, and your will and your wish."

Juan Diego left knowing he had not accomplished his mission. On the same day, he returned to Tepeyac, and she again appeared to him. He asked the lady to send "one of the more valuable nobles, a well-known people, one who is respected and esteemed" to be the messenger. But the lady insisted that he was the one. So, the next day, Sunday, Juan Diego again went to the palace to see the bishop. This time, the bishop told him that he could not proceed on her wishes just on the basis of his word and message. A sign from her would be necessary for him to believe that Juan Diego was indeed sent by the Lady from Heaven. He left once again without accomplishing his mission.

When Juan Diego returned home, he discovered that one of his uncles, named Juan Bernardino, had caught the smallpox and was in his last moments. Through the night, his uncle begged him to go to Tlatilolco to call a priest to come and hear his confession before he died. Juan Diego did not return that day to the lady for a sign that he had promised to bring to the bishop. Instead, he went to look for a priest the next day. He took another path in order to avoid meeting the lady, whom he thought would delay him from getting a priest before his uncle died. Yet the lady came down from the top of the hill and blocked his passage, and standing in front of him, said, "Where are you going?"

Juan Diego explained his uncle's situation. The lady assured him that his uncle was already healed and that he should not worry. She then instructed him to climb to the top of the hill where he had seen her before, cut and gather many diverse flowers, and bring them to her. He did as she instructed and was deeply surprised to find all kinds of exquisite flowers from Castile, because it was December, not a time for flowers. He gathered them and placed them in the hollow of his mantle. He took the flowers to the lady, who said, "These different flowers are the proof, the sign, that you will take to the bishop. In my name tell him that he is to see in them what I want, and with this he should carry out my wish and my will." He was further instructed to only open his mantle in the presence of the bishop.

Juan Diego took the flowers to the palace and again, with great difficulty, he finally got to see the bishop. He told the bishop everything that had happened and that he did bring a sign, as the bishop had demanded. "He unfolded his white mantle…and at that instant the different flowers from Castile fell to the ground. In that very moment she painted herself; the precious image of the Ever-Virgin Holy Mary, Mother of God Teotl, appeared suddenly, just as she is today and is kept in her precious home, in her hermitage of Tepeyac, which is called Guadalupe."

When the bishop saw her, he and all who accompanied him fell to their knees and were greatly astonished. He prayed to her and begged her to forgive him for not having believed her will, her heart, and her word. He immediately started the building of her temple. When Juan Diego returned home, he discovered that the lady had appeared to his uncle and had healed him.

The first time I read the whole story, I had an image of Juan Diego doing what he was told, walking back and forth every week from his home to the church in the city to receive his instructions—a prescribed way of life according to the conquerors of his people. And on that December evening, he was interrupted by the appearance of the Lady of Guadalupe. He was invited to take a Sabbath, which began with following the songs of the birds and later the signs of the flowers. Through his experience of encountering the Lady of Guadalupe, he was raised up from a lowly poor Indian into the messenger of the Divine, delivering a message that would change the history of the Americas. In the Náhuatl tradition, "flower and song" represent the truth.

> The Náhuatl theologians stated: "It may be that no one on earth can tell the truth, except through flower and song." Rational discourse clarifies yet limits the mind, while flowers and song stimulate the imagination to ponder the infinite. For the Náhuatl, it was only through poetic communication and beauty that the heart of human beings could enter into communion and communication with the divine—both individually and collectively. For the Náhuatl, truth was expressed through the suggestive harmony of the seen and heard. Through the beauty of the image (flowers) and the melodious sounds (poetic word), the divine could be gradually experienced, and one could gradually come to share in the divine wisdom.[4]

Sabbath is a time to learn and experience the truth for the powerless. This truth disputes the incomplete reality projected by the powerful in society. Through songs and flowers, Juan Diego learned the truth that he was beloved by God even though he and his people were conquered and powerless and were on the verge of dying spiritually, as symbolized by his dying uncle.

On the other hand, the bishop, representing the powerful conquerors, did not have the time for Juan Diego—he did not make time for Sabbath, when he could step out of his prescribed power role to truly encounter the powerless Indians. This was one of the reasons why the church was not successful in evangelizing to the Indians. They might all be baptized and seem faithful on the outside by coming for instructions from the church, but spiritually they were still a broken people. The story of Juan Diego teaches us that the powerful often will not listen unless the powerless persist in making themselves known. After the second rejection by the

---

[4]Ibid., 34–35.

bishop, Juan Diego, under the pressure of a dying uncle, almost gave up his empowered state and returned to the submissive, conquered state of being. He was doing what he was told by the powerful again—to go find a priest to give the last rites to his dying uncle. He even tried to avoid meeting the Lady of Guadalupe. He was avoiding Sabbath.

But she once again intervened and found Juan Diego. She insisted that he take his Sabbath and collect flowers for her—the truth—instead of going to find a priest to prepare for his uncle's death. Honoring Sabbath is about finding truth and life, not death. The sabbatical detour that Juan Diego took gave him the courage to confront the powerful with the truth again, even though the powerful were not ready to hear him. His persistence was based on his empowerment in knowing the truth: that he was beloved by God. At the crossing of the powerful and the powerless, the conquerors and the conquered, the Guadalupe event enabled the truth to come through. Together, the powerful and the powerless worked together to create a new future.

The pedagogy of the powerless began with learning the truth and, in the process, being empowered to act. A key part of the process is the preparation they need to do before they can encounter and challenge the powerful. This preparation involves learning the truth about their real reality and that they are blessed. They, in effect, become the messengers, bringing the good news that will transform the situation for both the powerful and the powerless, leading to a new creation.

Much has been written about the pedagogy of the powerless, particularly in Paulo Freire's classic book *A Pedagogy of the Oppressed*. In the theological circle, liberation theology is an accepted field of theological study supporting this pedagogical process. The pedagogy of the powerless, unlike the pedagogy of the powerful, may begin informally. As a teacher, you are already a suspect—are you one of them, the powerful? Can you be trusted? The development of trust is essential if the teacher is to be effective in working with the powerless. The following is a summary of the process for the pedagogy of the powerless based on my own experience in working with the powerless:

1.   Create a gracious environment in which the powerless can find a community of support.[5] This may include inviting people to gather informally for community building, then having a more formal meeting for studying the Holy Scriptures together and sharing concerns and prayers.

2.   Once the trust is developed, find ways to enable the people to articulate and describe their experience of the real reality—their experienced truth—as distinct from what the powerful in society have put forth as the truth. Tools such as Photolanguage and other group media would be useful here.[6]

3.   If they are not able to articulate clearly their experience by themselves, help them organize the information and re-present it back to the community. Do not impose your interpretation of the reality on them. The students must be considered as "critical co-investigators in dialogue with the teacher. The teacher presents the material to the students for their consideration, and re-considers her [or his] earlier considerations as the students express their own."[7] This is a mutual learning process. Paulo Freire called this way of teaching "problem-posing" education in which "the teacher is no longer merely the-one-who-teaches, but one who is himself [or herself] taught in dialogue with the students, who in turn while being taught also teach. They become jointly responsible for a process in which all grow."[8] The goal is using the resources, skills, knowledge, and experiences of the community in their fullness to describe the problem or issue together, putting together the different pieces in ways that can be articulated, shared, and affirmed.

4.   Doing Bible study each time they gather is essential for the empowerment process. Consistently point out how God and Christ interact with the poor and powerless in

---

[5]Again, see Law, *Inclusion,* for specific techniques in creating a "grace margin."

[6]For techniques in enabling a group to articulate themselves through different kinds of "group media," see Law, *The Wolf Shall Dwell,* 89–98.

[7]Paulo Freire, *A Pedagogy of the Oppressed* (New York: Continuum, 1970), 62.

[8]Ibid., 61.

the Bible. Make correlations between the biblical story and their own stories. Ask these questions: How does God through Christ see the situation that you are in? What does God invite you to do? As the community begins to differentiate between God's will and the real reality of their situation, the movement toward change begins.

5. After articulating their real reality and putting it next to the pattern of truth put forth by the gospel, they might discover the real issues, and they may mobilize to take action to change their own situation. Here, you may help in creating and bringing them to the crossing to articulate their concerns to the powerful. This movement implies that you have the ability and influence to work with the powerful to prepare them for the crossing. As a teacher, you might need to coordinate this with teachers working with the pedagogy of the powerful to carefully plan the encounter at the crossing.

6. If the powerful are not ready or willing to listen, the powerless must continue to empower one another. They must learn to tell their side of the story, raising the tension without buying into the destructive political ways of the world. That is, do not play the power game, and do not incite violence, which would give the powerful more reasons to counterattack. The powerless need to empower one another to be persistent and to insist on being heard—like Juan Diego insisted on seeing the bishop time and again to deliver his message—while not participating in supporting the old system (in which Juan Diego would need to find a priest to say the last rite for his uncle). The civil rights movement in the United States led by Dr. Martin Luther King, Jr., followed this process, with people protesting nonviolently, articulating the injustices experienced by the powerless, raising the tension, and refusing to continue to support the oppressive system through boycotting and civil disobedience. Eventually, the powerful come to realize that the system does not work without the support of the powerless and may decide to listen. Then, you work to set up the encounter—the crossing.

7.   The process at the crossing can take many forms. The careful preparation of the powerless to articulate the truth is a key part of the empowerment process. By the time they gather to dialogue, the powerless must be ready to speak their truth, and the powerful must be ready to listen. The design of these gatherings has to be well thought out, ensuring that both the powerful and the powerless are entering into the grace margin. All my previous books were devoted to the theology and the practical skills of how to create such an environment.

8.   Having spoken their truthful words, all are then invited to listen to the reflections of the others. Let the dialogue continue.

9.   Having listened to one another, the whole community— both the powerful and powerless—discuss what they can do to transform their lives into a community moving closer to God's will.

In any given diverse community, there will be power differentiations among the different groups. In all of the diversity dimensions—age, race, ethnicity, gender, sexual orientation, ability, and so forth—one group is almost always perceived to be more powerful than the others. Teaching in the crossings of these differences requires us, first, to be aware of the power differentiations.[9] This perception of power often changes according to the environment. For example, in most situations between older and younger people, the older people are considered more powerful. However, if we are dealing with how to use a computer and other new technologies, the younger people might be considered more powerful than the older people. Being able to do power analysis is then an essential skill for teaching at the crossings.

The teacher must know that the pedagogies of the powerful and the powerless are different. There will be a difference in preparing them to enter the crossing in order to encounter one another for the purpose of discovering the truth. There are different skills involved. For example, when working with the powerful, the teacher must know how to negotiate for time and

---

[9]"Power analysis" is another essential technique for leadership in a multicultural community. See Law, *The Wolf Shall Dwell,* 45–52.

how to gain commitment to honor Sabbath. When working with the powerless, the teacher must gain trust first, sometimes in an informal way, in the context of a community. At the crossing, the teacher must carefully facilitate the process of truth-telling, beginning with the powerless, while inviting the powerful to listen first. Then the dialogue must continue. More importantly, all this must be done in the context of the gospel of Jesus Christ.

Teaching and proclaiming the good news of Jesus Christ is a political act. Following Christ's pattern, we facilitate a power shift between the powerful and the powerless. This power shift is the beginning of our discernment of the truth. We must pay even more attention to what happens after the power shift has occurred, because Christ's political action does not follow the political pattern of the world. We must continue our work so that we do not fall into the world's destructive political pattern. The long history of power shifts in different nations has retold many times the destructive pattern in which revolutionaries, acting on behalf of the powerless, take up power and then proceed to persecute those who had been powerful. It is a continuation of the destructive cycle of violence and domination. The good news of Jesus Christ affects the power shift, but Christ also calls on us not to take part in the way of the world's destructive pattern.

> *"You know that among the Gentiles those whom they recognize as their rulers lord it over them, and their great ones are tyrants over them. But it is not so among you; but whoever wishes to become great among you must be your servant, and whoever wishes to be first among you must be slave of all. For the Son of man came not to be served but to serve, and to give his life a ransom for many." (Mk. 10:42b–45)*

In the crossings of the powerful and the powerless, Christ calls us to live a new pattern of life that is different from the world's cycle of domination. Christ calls us to live in the peaceable realm of God, in which the wolf shall dwell with the lamb, and the lion and the calf can live in harmony. The presence of Christ puts us in a new state of being with one another—one that is based on abundance instead of scarcity, love and compassion instead of condemnation, justice instead of vengeance, forgiveness instead of holding grudges. As we do our parts as teachers to facilitate the power shifts and the continuing dialogue, we must put the gospel at the center of everything that we do. This can be done through preaching and the regular discipline of studying the Holy Scriptures together. We must have the constant reminder that it is not we who transform the world, but God. Yes, we will do our parts the best we can, but in the end, it is the gospel that affirms, confronts, and converts people. It is the gospel of Jesus Christ that gives the courage for the powerful to let go of control, to open up their boundaries, to honor Sabbath. It is the gospel of Jesus Christ that affirms the blessedness of the powerless and empowers them to articulate their experienced truth and to take action to challenge the powerful. It is the gospel of Jesus Christ that calls us to find a new way to be in community that does not follow the destructive patterns of the world. It is the *Word* that is the *truth* that will transform us into a new creation at the crossings of our lives.

Chapter 8

Christmas at the Crossings: A Play

I would like to end this book on a lighter note with a play called "Rudolph and the Little Lamb." This is a Christmas play I wrote a few years ago that was professionally produced as part of a Festival of Faith in Los Angeles in 2001 by Cornerstone Theater Company. I include the play because I believe that this play captures some of what I have been trying to describe in this book. Enjoy.

Rudolph and the Little Lamb—A Play

(Christmas Eve. "Rudolph the Red-Nosed Reindeer" is heard in the background. On a rooftop, surrounded by lights, is a reindeer, RUDOLPH, with a red light bulb for a nose. The structure on which he stands is supported by, on one side, the edge of the roof and, on the other side, a wood pole extended all the way to the ground. At the foot of the pole is a little lamb, BABA. He is part of a modest nativity display. RUDOLPH is humming his song.)

BABA   Cool it, Rudolph! I'm sick of that song.

RUDOLPH   Baba! You're just jealous because you don't have a
            song of your own.

BABA   That's not...

RUDOLPH   Oh, I'm sorry. I take that back. You *do* have a song.
            (Sings.) Baba Black Sheep have you any wool? Yes sir,
            yes sir, three bags full.

135

BABA　　　　Rudolph, shut up!

RUDOLPH　　But what kind of a song is that? It has absolutely nothing to do with Christmas.

BABA　　　　Because it's not a Christmas song!

RUDOLPH　　Then why are you here if you have nothing to do with Christmas?

BABA　　　　Because… *(Searches for an answer.)* I'm here to stop you from singing that stupid song.

RUDOLPH　　Ha! Just how are you gonna do that?

(RUDOLPH starts singing his song again.)

BABA　　　　Stop! Stop! What about the children?!

RUDOLPH　　The children? They love me.

BABA　　　　They love you!?

RUDOLPH　　You just can't stand it when the children love me more than they love you.

BABA　　　　I don't care if they love me or not. I just don't want them to…get confused over what Christmas is about.

RUDOLPH　　What's there's to be confused about? Christmas is about Santa Claus, my boss, giving…

BABA　　　　No, Christmas is about the birth of Jesus.

RUDOLPH　　Yeah, right. Does your little Jesus fly on Christmas Eve and give little children toys, making them very happy everywhere?

BABA　　　　No. But little Jesus gives much more than that.

RUDOLPH　　Like what? He can hardly walk or talk. Look at him, so helpless.

BABA　　　　No. But when he grows up, he's gonna give his life to save the whole world.

RUDOLPH   Now, how long is that gonna take? Twenty? Thirty years? I can't wait that long. The little children can't wait that long. By the time your little Jesus grows up and hires a bunch of reindeer to deliver toys, the little children are all grown up. In case you didn't notice, grown-ups don't play with toys.

BABA   Jesus isn't gonna grow up to be a Santa Claus. He's gonna die for us all. That's what the shepherds told me.

RUDOLPH   This is Christmas time! You can't go around telling little children that this baby's gonna die! That would scare them.

BABA   Of course I can't. But…

RUDOLPH   Let me tell you what Christmas is really about from my personal experience. Christmas is about recognizing that everyone can have the potential to out-shine everybody else—like me and my nose. Christmas is about having your dream come true, becoming the leader, being number one. Christmas is about proving to all those who laughed at you that they were wrong, and if they're to keep their jobs as Santa's reindeer, they had better start loving me. Because I'm the beloved one.

BABA   Oh, my God! That's the opposite of what Christmas is all about!

RUDOLPH   If that is the case, why am I up here with all the lights and you're down there in that dark little dirty shack?

BABA   Because…because…I don't know. I'm just a lamb. All I know is that there are always little lambs sitting by little Jesus at Christmas. So they just put me here. I have no idea what I'm supposed to do!

RUDOLPH   That's why you're jealous—you're having a identity crisis. Not me. I know exactly who I am: Rudolph the Red-Nosed Reindeer!

(He sings his song again.)

BABA	*(To the other statues.)* Mary? Joseph? Say something. You can say it so much better than me. Tell him what Christmas is really about. C'mon, shepherds, angels, why don't you say something? Say something! Anything! *(Silence. BABA is frustrated.)* Sometimes I wish you guys could be more like Santa Claus— bright colors, bright lights, flying above everything, seeing everything, knowing everything. I wish I could fly.
RUDOLPH	*(Mocking.)* What about the angels? They have wings. Maybe they can take you for a ride? How about a race? C'mon angels, I'll race you to the moon! Ha! Ha! Ha!
BABA	Rudolph, you know those angels don't fly. All they do is sit there with their stupid horns that don't make noise. Maybe this whole thing is a joke. Maybe there's no Jesus! Maybe there's no peace on earth. Maybe there's no Son of God! Maybe there's no God at all!

(Silence.)

RUDOLPH	I'll tell you what. Next time I fly Santa to deliver the toys, why don't you come along?
BABA	Really? You don't think Santa would mind?
RUDOLPH	Mind? He's the jolliest of them all. He's so good that he didn't even mind that we were beating each other up just to get his attention.
BABA	Shouldn't he have stopped that?
RUDOLPH	Well, he just, you know, likes to see only the good things in life. According to my story, he didn't even notice that the other reindeer were laughing at me until he needed me on that foggy Christmas night.
BABA	I'm sorry.

RUDOLPH	Sorry for what?
BABA	For what you've gone through.
RUDOLPH	Hey, no pain, no gain. I'm here, am I not? I can't wait 'til Santa comes to take us for the ride.
BABA	So when are we gonna take off?
RUDOLPH	Pretty soon. It's Christmas Eve.
BABA	What time?
RUDOLPH	When Santa shows up.
BABA	When's that?
RUDOLPH	I don't know.
BABA	How can you not know? You're Rudolph, the leader of the reindeer.
RUDOLPH	I'll let you know when it's time.
BABA	Haven't you flown for Santa before?
RUDOLPH	Eh…yes, of course.
BABA	When did he show up last time?
RUDOLPH	I don't know. When it starts snowing, I guess.
BABA	What if it doesn't snow?
RUDOLPH	Maybe when the wind starts blowing.
BABA	Why do you need the wind?
RUDOLPH	That's obvious. Have you ever seen the leaves fly? They only fly when the wind is blowing. That's how I'm gonna fly.
BABA	What if the wind doesn't blow?
RUDOLPH	You sound like one of those stupid lambs from the fairy tales. Don't ask so many stupid questions!
BABA	But I need to get ready. I need to say goodbye to Mary and Joseph and the shepherds and little Jesus.

RUDOLPH   Baba, you're so sentimental. When you're in the Christmas business, you can't be too sentimental about seeing kids happy or saying goodbye and stuff like that, or you'll never finish delivering the toys in one night.

(Silence.)

BABA   Are you sure there's a Santa Claus?

RUDOLPH   Nonsense!

BABA   You've never even seen him.

RUDOLPH   Of course I have. He wears a red suit. He has a big white beard. He…

BABA   You've been up there for three weeks now. I never saw him visiting you or feeding you or anything like that.

RUDOLPH   Well…he's a very busy man!

BABA   Rudolph. Tell me the truth.

(A strong wind starts to blow.)

RUDOLPH   Whee! I told you so. When the wind starts blowing, I'm gonna fly! I'm gonna fly!

BABA   Stop moving, Rudolph, the pole's coming loose!

RUDOLPH   Whee, whee! Santa's coming to get me, and I'm gonna help him deliver toys to all the little…Oh, no!

(He's off-balance because the wind is stronger now.)

BABA   Stop moving or the pole's gonna fall!

RUDOLPH   I'm *not* moving!

BABA   Why is the pole still shaking then?

RUDOLPH   I don't know…The wind!

BABA   Start flying then. The pole's not gonna hold up too long with this wind.

(RUDOLPH holds on to the structure, afraid and paralyzed.)

BABA   For God's sake, start flying, Rudolph!

RUDOLPH   I don't know how!

BABA   I thought all reindeer knew how to fly.

RUDOLPH   I've never tried it.

BABA   Then how did you help Santa deliver the toys?

RUDOLPH   I've never met Santa! I only knew the story when the children sang that song!

BABA   Why did you lie to me?

RUDOLPH   I don't know! I just want to be somebody!

(Another strong gust of wind.)

              Oh, my God! I'm gonna fall! I'm gonna die, and I'll never get to see Santa!

(BABA stands as tall as he can and holds the pole steady with all his strength.)

BABA   Don't worry, Rudolph, I've got it!

RUDOLPH   That's good. What did you do?

BABA   *(To self.)* God! Help me! Give me strength!

(The wind persists.)

RUDOLPH   Don't let go! Baba, don't let go!

BABA   I won't let go! I won't!

RUDOLPH   Baba, you're my best friend in the whole world, and I'll never forget you. When Santa comes, I'll tell him what you've done, and he'll definitely take you along to deliver the toys. Who knows, he might put you in charge of all the elves.

(The wind finally stops. Silence.)

              Thank God the wind has stopped. You know, Baba, do you think Santa was testing us with that wind?—to see if we can really do our jobs? Baba! Are you there?

(He looks down and sees BABA *lying motionless under a toppled Christmas tree.)*

> Baba! Answer me! Baba! Oh, my God! Baba! Don't leave me! Who's gonna talk to me now? I'm sorry I made you feel bad. Why? God, why?

(He cries.)

(Silence. The church bells are ringing. RUDOLPH *looks at* BABA, *looks at the baby Jesus in the manger, and then looks back to* BABA *again. He hears children singing "What Child Is This?" in the distance.* RUDOLPH'S *tears fall on* BABA'S *head.* BABA *wakes.)*

BABA   Rudolph? Rudolph? Are you okay?

RUDOLPH   Baba! You're alive! You're alive!

BABA   Why are you crying?

RUDOLPH   I thought you got hit by that tree and…Anyway, I'm so glad you're alive!

BABA   What happened? I was holding this pole. I wasn't gonna let go no matter what. Then everything turned black. I couldn't see any light. I couldn't move. It's like I…

RUDOLPH   Fainted. That tree hit you and you fainted.

BABA   Then I saw the face of a man. He was, like, all beat up. He was weak like he was dying. Then I heard a voice, and it said, "This is Jesus. Listen to him."

RUDOLPH   That's weird.

BABA   Then this man said, "Forgive them; for they don't know what they're doing." Then I kept hearing in my head over and over again: "Forgive them; for they don't know what they're doing."

RUDOLPH & BABA Forgive them; for they don't know what they're doing.

BABA   Then I felt this wetness on my head. I looked up, and I saw you crying.

RUDOLPH   You know, I think that's what Christmas is really about.

BABA   You think so?

RUDOLPH   Yeah, Christmas is about what you've done for me.

BABA   What have I done?

RUDOLPH   You risked your life to save my life!

BABA   No, I was just…

RUDOLPH   And you forgave me even though I was mean to you.

BABA   Forgave you!?

RUDOLPH   Yeah, why else would you want to save me?

BABA   You're my friend.

RUDOLPH   Really?! You think I'm your friend?

BABA   Yes, you're my friend, and I don't care whether you can fly or not. I'm just glad that you're alive.

RUDOLPH   I'm glad that you're alive too.

(They hear children singing "Joy to the World" in the distance. BABA and RUDOLPH sing along joyfully.)

The End

Appendix

Preparation Process for Preaching in a Multicontextual Community

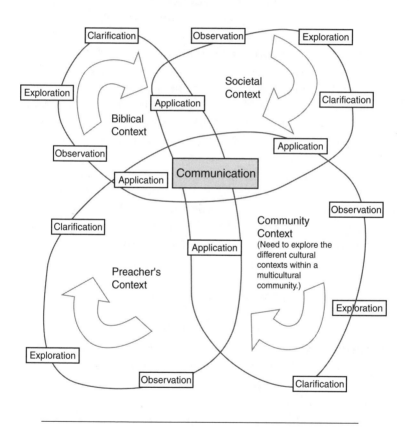

The following process is a systematic approach to discovering ideas, themes, stories, concepts, or arguments that might be useful in preparing a sermon to be preached in a multicontextual community. For a visual image of what this process involves, review the diagram on the previous page. You can begin at any one of the four loops, as long as you move through all four in the process. For example, if something major happened within your faith community this week, you might want to begin your exploration with the Community Context first. If you are struggling with a particular issue this week, you might want to start with the Preacher's Context first. In any case, read the biblical text(s) for the sermon, especially for those of you who follow a lectionary, and then proceed from one of the loops following the line.

Notice that each loop takes you through a similar reflection process with the following sections: Observation, Exploration, Clarification, Application, and Communication. In the Application and Communication sections, as you follow the line, you will be walking through two other loops before going to a more in-depth exploration of the next loop. If one of these areas evokes some energy or interest in you, go to that loop. You don't have to follow the sequence of exploration as layed out in these worksheets.

I have provided a list of questions for each loop. The questions are to lead you through the exploration of each context. You do not have to have an answer to each question. If the question does not apply, move on. If the question does not help you gain any more insights, move on. The key is to move through all four areas of reflection before putting together your sermon. Usually, when you have worked through all four areas of reflection, the Application and Communication segments of each of the areas will provide you with more than enough ideas to construct a sermon.

The Biblical Context

OBSERVATION
- Clear your mind of any previous ideas about the Bible text. Read the text aloud. Have a moment of silence. What are the images, words, phrases that stay with you in the silence?
- What is the literary form/genre of this text?
- Take some time to look at what goes before this text. What comes after? What is the function of this text in the context of the book from which it came?
- Read the text again, keeping the literary and contextual information in mind. Have another moment of silence.

EXPLORATION

- Is this text connected with or similar to another text in the Bible? See, for example, parallel stories in the four gospels, references to the Hebrew Scriptures, and so forth. How does this comparison of similar texts inform you of the intention of the author or about the intended audience of the text?
- What might be the cultural, political, socioeconomic, and theological contexts of the author?
- What might be the cultural, political, socioeconomic, and theological contexts of the intended audience?
- If the text describes a story with different players, what are the power relationships among the players? Where is God, or how does God act in the lives of the different players?

CLARIFICATION

- How does the exploration inform you about the meaning of this text for its intended audience? What does it challenge? What does it affirm? What does it call them to do?
- How does this text reveal the presence and action of God in the lives of individuals, the community, and the world?
- What is the good news?

APPLICATION

- In what ways does the meaning of this text inform and connect with the concerns and issues that you and your community face in the world today (the societal context)? What does it challenge? What does it affirm? What does it call you to do?
- In what ways does the meaning of this text inform and connect with the concerns and issues of your faith community (the community context)? What does it challenge? What does it affirm? What does it call you to do?
- In what ways does the meaning of this text inform and connect with your personal life (the preacher's context)? What event/experience/memory does this text evoke?

COMMUNICATION

- From this reflection, what story, theme, concept, argument, or idea might be appropriate to include for your preaching?

The Preacher's Context

OBSERVATION

- What is a recent event that has had a significant impact in your life?
- (If you have done the exploration of the biblical context first, what event/experience does this text bring forth in your memory?)
- Describe what happened.
- What did you see? What did you hear? What did you feel? How did you react?

EXPLORATION

- What caused you to react the way you did?
- Where does this reaction connect with your internal culture (your beliefs, values, assumptions, patterns, and myths)?
- Does it bring up another significant event in your past that you need to examine more? Why?

CLARIFICATION

- What new insight about yourself did you learn, especially about your internal culture?
- In this event, where was God, or how did God act in your life?
- What is the good news for you personally?

APPLICATION

- In what ways does your personal context connect with the biblical text, bringing forth the good news for contemporary life? What does it challenge? What does it affirm?
- In what ways does your personal context inform and connect with the concerns and issues that you and your community face in the world today? What does it challenge? What does it affirm?
- In what ways does your personal context inform and connect with the concerns and issues of the people in your faith community? What does it challenge? What does it affirm?

COMMUNICATION

- In your exploration of your personal context, what values, beliefs, assumptions, patterns, and myths have you discerned that are uniquely yours?
- How might these be different from your community's internal culture?

- How does this inform you of what personal information is appropriate to include in your preaching?
- In your exploration of your personal context, where is your passion for the good news? In what ways can you infuse your preaching with this passion?
- What story, theme, concept, argument, or idea from this reflection might be appropriate for use in your preaching for your community?

The Community Context

OBSERVATION

- What is a recent event that has had a significant impact in your community?
- (If you have done the exploration of the biblical context first, what community event/experience does this text bring forth in your memory?)
- Describe what happened. Describe a preceding event leading up to this experience. Describe also the proceeding reaction to this experience.
- Are there different reactions to the same event by different groups? Describe them separately. What did you see? What did you hear? (Stay with this behavior and try not to make any interpretations yet.)

EXPLORATION

- What caused people in your community to act and react in the ways they did?
- What information-seeking questions do you ask your community in order to get a better understanding of what happened from the different community perspectives?
- To whom do you need to listen in order to gain a deeper understanding of the different internal cultures of the community? If there are different groups in your community holding different perspectives, determine which group has less power and find ways to listen to that group first.

CLARIFICATION

- What values, beliefs, assumptions, patterns, or myths of your community did you discover from this exploration? Are there major differences among the different groups? What are they?

- Where was God, or how did God act in this event/experience for the different groups?
- What is the good news for your community?

APPLICATION

- What values, beliefs, assumptions, patterns, and myths have you discerned that might be unique to the different groups in your community? How might they be different or similar to your own internal culture?
- Do you share the same internal culture with your community? With which group? How does the answer to this question inform how you can better relate/affirm/challenge the people of your community?
- In what ways does the exploration of your community's contexts connect with the biblical text, bringing forth the good news for contemporary life? In what ways does the biblical text challenge or affirm the beliefs, values, assumptions, patterns, or myths of the different groups in your community?
- In what ways do your community's contexts inform and connect with the concerns and issues that they face in the world today (the societal context)? What does it challenge? What does it affirm?

COMMUNICATION

- In your exploration of your community's contexts, where is the passion of your community?
- In what ways does the biblical text connect/challenge/affirm this passion?
- If appropriate, in what ways can you tap into this passion in your preaching?
- What story, theme, concept, argument, or idea from this reflection might be appropriate for use in your preaching for your community?
- What experience from your personal context may be appropriate to use to help your community struggle with being faithful to the gospel?

The Societal Context

OBSERVATION

- What is a recent event in society or in the world that has had a significant impact on you and your community?
- (If you have done the exploration of the biblical context first, what recent societal event/experience does this text bring forth in your memory?)
- Describe what happened. Describe preceding events leading up to this experience. Describe also the proceeding reactions to this experience.
- Are there different reactions to the same event by different groups in society? Describe them separately. What did you see? What did you hear? (Stay with behavior and try not to make any interpretations yet.)

EXPLORATION

- What caused people in society to act and react in the ways they did?
- What research do you need to do in order to gain a better understanding of what happened from the societal point of view?
- To whom do you need to listen in order to gain a deeper understanding of the internal cultures of the different groups in the society in which your community resides? Listen to the powerless groups first.

CLARIFICATION

- What new insight did you learn about the society in which your community resides?
- What societal value, belief, pattern, or myth does this exploration bring out?
- Where was God, or how did God act in this event/experience?
- What is the good news for your society?

APPLICATION

- Do the people of your community share the same internal culture with society? With which group? How does the answer to this question inform how you can better relate/affirm/challenge the people of your community through your preaching?

- Do you share the same internal culture with society? With which group? How does the answer to this question inform how you can better relate/affirm/challenge the people of your community through your preaching?
- In what ways does the societal context connect with the biblical text bringing forth the good news for contemporary life? In what ways does the biblical text challenge or affirm the values, beliefs, assumptions, patterns, or myths of the different groups in society?

COMMUNICATION
- Where is the passion of the different groups in society?
- How does the gospel challenge or affirm this passion?
- If appropriate, in what ways can you tap into this passion in your preaching?
- What story, concept, argument, or idea from this reflection might be appropriate for use in your preaching for your community?

Having walked through all four areas of reflection, you can go back and review the Communication and Application sections from all four areas. Verbalize the materials noted in your responses. Tell the stories. Expound on the themes. Crystallize the poetic images. Flesh out the ideas.

Then have a time of silence.

Pray for the Holy Spirit to inspire you to construct and preach a sermon that will connect the members of your community with God and with one another; a sermon that will help them make sense of the multicultural world in which we live; a sermon that will empower them to act faithfully, justly, and compassionately in the world.